Here and Hereafter
FOREVER AFTER

The 9th Plane of Heaven

JEANNE REJAUNIER

Copyright © 2017 Jeanne Rejaunier

All rights reserved.

ISBN-13: 978-1981652150

ISBN-10: 1981652159

DEDICATION

To the memory of beautiful soul and beloved friend,
Hollywood actress Francine York.

CONTENTS

Dedication
Acknowledgments
Preface
Introduction
Maps

Part I

The Plateau between the 8th & 9th Planes
Review I
The 9th Plane
Review II

Part II

Stations Of The Steeps 1-12
Other 9th Plane temples
Reviews III-XV

Part III

About Mary Weddell
Author Jeanne Rejaunier Bio
Planes of Heaven reviews
Other books by Jeanne Rejaunier
Reviews of The Beauty Trap
Gallery

JEANNE REJAUNIER

ACKNOWLEDGMENTS

Abundant thanks to the eternal lives of those who shared our Friday classes and our nighttime adventures on the Planes of Heaven with our beloved Mary Weddell and her devoted assistant, Miriam Willis: Glenn Dies, Violet Stevens, Connie Smith, Margaret Branchflower, Yvonne (Vonnie) and John Branchflower, Miriam Albplanalp, Esther Barnes, Esther and Bill Estabrook, Gertrude and Linda Clark, George Flournoy, Dr. Fred Adler, Christine Adler (aka Carmen Austin); Sylvia and Andrew Howe, Elizabeth Kirby, Ruth Thomas, Ruth Taylor, Ruth and Frank Crandall, Rowena and Ralph Meeks; Barbara, Willard and Jennifer Stone; Diana Davis, Jack Spahr, Katie and John Basinski; Grace Hale; Dale, Mary Jean, Beth, and John Cope; Lola Grube, Patti Chalgren, Emily Rosebrough, Alma Johnson, Lenore, Ruby Perkins, Frances, Doris, Kathy, Marilyn, Sandra, Henriette Kohrsler, Helen and Ed von Gehr, Helen Marsh, Helen Flatwed, Helen DeCant, Bernard Burry, Ellen King, Shelley O'Day, Lee Merrin, Eve Bruce, Judith Porter, Evelyn Swanson, Mary Werti, the three Virginias (Anderson, Lockwood, and (?); Louise Eggleston, Louise Cabral; Eleanor, Elizabeth, Eva Totah, Jane Wright, Nita, Rosemary, Kathy, Woodie, Avis, Amy, Ida, Lorna Lane, Hank, Dan, Gene Haffner, Richard, Robert, Michael, Carol, Pat Settles, Ann, Joanne, Lu Ann Horstman, Marlu Been-Swan; June Walters, Frieda, Lois, Ethel, Dorothy Harvel; Bill and Clara Jackson, Margie Brown, and everyone else I may have missed who shared the beautiful evenings in Pasadena and nighttimes in the Planes of Heaven - some with us still, others now living on the Other Side, in one world without end, Amen.

PREFACE

****

Here and Hereafter - Forever After is the seventh book in the Planes of Heaven series. The first six titles took readers from Heaven's planes up through the 8th Plane. We now begin our travels to the Plateau between the 8th and 9th Planes, then "climb" to the 9th Plane of Heaven, as we continue a higher octave of themes begun in the previous Planes books with added new emphasis. As spiritual seekers, ours is an endless journey of progression, during which realizations bring greater integration within than ever before, as we grasp further ties to that invisible world beyond the physical life we know and live.

Man has long sought a key to the mysteries of the origin and destiny of who we are, where we came from and where we're going. What occurs when we reach the end of this earthly life to which we have become so accustomed and attached? What awaits us at the transition of death? Do we still exist? Are we conscious? Will we rejoin loved ones who have preceded us to another realm? What is it like over there? How can we best prepare for our inevitable departure from here to there? Many ways, many masters, and degrees of scientific understanding have been employed to discover how to reach the invisible Other Side of life, the next world, the Afterlife, to determine how to relate to it, and what we can do now to understand our place in it.

In previous Planes of Heaven titles, we noted the surging popularity of books about life after death, Heaven and the Afterlife. Information contained in the majority of these works, we observed, is largely based on reports by individuals undergoing near death experiences (NDE); mediums channeling guides and discarnates from the Other Side; automatic writing; and anecdotal evidence from past life regressions, including subjects under hypnosis. To this list let us add cryptic biblical passages, along with their differing interpretations, the precise meanings of which have engaged man over millennia.

As readers of the Planes series know, the unique material described in the Planes of Heaven books is of a different source than any of the above. It derives from the experiences of a group of some fifty to sixty seekers who, for a period of decades, met Friday evenings in Pasadena, California, under the guidance of our mentor, master teacher and Dead Sea Scrolls translator Mary Dies Weddell, whose extensive knowledge of ancient languages (Sanskrit, Hebrew, Aramaic, Latin, Greek, hieroglyphics), esoteric truth and inspired teachings influenced thousands in America and abroad. While many elements mentioned in other books on heaven and the afterlife are corroborated in the Planes material, our Pasadena group ventured into areas unexplored in other books.

One of Mary Weddell's spiritual gifts was the ability to take her students to the Other Side in their sleep at night for spiritual training, and then help us recall our experiences. Having mastered laws governing the ascent and descent of the soul between Heaven and Earth, with the help of invisible hosts, Mary summoned our spiritual bodies as we slept, allowing us to enter the higher realms, to be met by guides and teachers from the Other Side for night teaching in the heaven world's temples and halls of learning. When Mary made her transition, our nighttime sojourns continued.

As the Planes of Heaven series of books examine life in the invisible world, we see how intricately interconnected are our physical existence on Earth and the realms beyond; in the process, we see how visiting the heavens in our sleep prepares us for the Afterlife, increases our spiritual awareness, and enriches our lives in the here and now, helping us to understand why we have incarnated into this Earth school.

Throughout history, parallel teachings of major cultures have taught night travel in sleep as a way of gaining priceless spiritual insights, wisdom and understanding. This same ancient path enabled those of us in the Pasadena classes to be exposed to the heavenly temples and halls of learning, and to bring back vivid experiences and detailed descriptions of the heavenworld we experienced.

Through two powerful original courses, Creative Color Analysis and the Planes of Heaven, our teacher Mary enabled us, her students, to see more deeply into ourselves and to better understand the awe inspiring structure and purpose of creation. In these studies, Mary was assisted by senior teacher Miriam B. Willis, whose gentle and loving presence appears throughout this book as well as in the previous six titles of the Planes of Heaven series.

In Mary's words: "Somewhere in the great pool of knowledge that lies in eternity are the answers to all things the human heart so longs to learn, and sometimes the human mind awakens to seeking. It is my greatest desire to be of service, to express my deepest self in the world of mortals, that I may perhaps help someone find his way. I do not care in which direction I am sent, as long as it is the will of my Creator, and as long as I may serve. This is my purpose in existing, my goal in life as well as in death. If it is my destiny to be a channel for any of the knowledge which will contribute to the awareness of man, then I am deeply grateful.

"Ofttimes you read in great literature where man came out of the darkness into the light of understanding, into a worshipful awareness of who he is, how he came to be here, where he's going. Why is he here, and where does he go from here? That is the question on the soul of every living creature. They're wondering: why this life? What is this life for? Why are we going along, accumulating masses for some and nothing for others? Why is there suffering? Why hatred? Why so much selfishness and misunderstanding?

"In my teaching, I believe the only solution to the mysteries of man's existence and of his everyday toiling toward a goal he does not fully understand is to seek the inner self. Answers are waiting to every question concerning eternity, the material life and all phases of creation. All spiritual truth comes from the same ancient source; therefore it is a matter of awakening awareness, of developing dormant consciousness. Each man must become aware of his place in creation. You cannot falter or fail in any way because you are beautiful, a living proof there is a God."

*****

INTRODUCTION

Color ... "the Channel" ... the Planes of Heaven ... nighttime soul travel ... the silver cord ... the Sleep World ... temples ... tests ... "lions"... development ... the Eightfold Path ...

These words are familiar terms Mary Weddell's students. What do they mean to someone hearing them for the first time, or to the reader who gleans only a vague notion of what they are? In our Friday evening Planes of Heaven classes, review was a frequent feature, both to orient newcomers to the group, as well as to more firmly implant teachings in our own consciousness. In the spirit of this tradition, we will briefly define a few key topics so that new readers will feel comfortable with their meanings, and readers who have followed the books in the Planes series will have their minds refreshed, as we begin at the Plateau between the 8th and 9th Planes, then proceed to the 9th Plane itself.

THE PLANES OF HEAVEN The Planes are both a consciousness within and a heavenly locale. Think of them as illustrating vibratory rates and dimensions of reality in the invisible world where our spiritual bodies dwelled prior to physical incarnation, where we will once again inhabit in the hereafter, and which we can access every night in sleep while we are living on Earth.

NIGHTTIME SOUL TRAVEL During sleep, everyone "goes" somewhere, whether to the heavenly Planes for spiritual development, or to the Sleep World for rest.

THE SLEEP WORLD A rest area for souls who are not in spiritual work on the Planes. Dreams experienced by the soul and filtered to the intelligence of the dreamer may often stimulate and inspire the dreamer to pursue spiritual training in the temples and halls of learning on the Planes of Heaven.

TEMPLES AND HALLS OF LEARNING Every plane of the heaven world has many temples and halls of learning where, guided by heavenly teachers as our physical bodies sleep, spiritual seekers examine, evaluate and seek to improve our lives. We see ourselves through mirrors in which we view our faults and errors, and determine how to make changes in our lives to reach the next level in ongoing development. Our night work not only strengthens our ties to the invisible world, but may also reunite us with loved ones who have preceded us to the Afterlife.

THE SILVER CORD When we contact that other world every night in sleep, our spiritual bodies are connected to our physical bodies by the spiritual cord, also known as the silver cord. This cord is attenuated when traveling out of the body; it is extended during night work on the Planes, and severed only at death.

TESTS Tests are given us in the temples to cleanse negativity we need to clear. Tests on spiritual planes precede and parallel ones in the physical world, and are a means of unfolding consciousness, enabling us to grow in wisdom and understanding.

COLOR The Color path is a mystical journey toward soul development. Mary's color teaching, embodied in her Creative Color Analysis course, is unlike any other color system. It is a beautiful path of spiritual development, a way of changing and transforming ourselves. From an advanced state of consciousness, Mary brought through from the Other Side more than one hundred fully tested color rays and their definitions that form the basis of her unique Color course, a complement to her work on the Planes of Heaven. These colors consist of four Psychological and five Spiritual Arcs of 12 rays each (108 rays), plus a number of extended spiritual rays.

KEYNOTE COLOR The keynote color is the topmost color in aura, above the head. As we grow spiritually, the spiritual aura expands and the keynote color reaches higher and wider.

THE CHANNEL The Channel, also known as the Channel of our Being and the Keys to the Kingdom, comprising twelve spiritual colors, is our spiritual connection between the Earth plane and higher states of consciousness. This inner portion of a human being is the path of light leading one's consciousness to greater realms of understanding.

THE EIGHTFOLD PATH The Eightfold Path is generally associated with Gautama Buddha, who rediscovered this ancient teaching taught for thousands of years by all previous Buddhas. Buddhists refer to the "Noble Eightfold Path," the fourth of the Buddha's Four Noble Truths, incorporating the practices of right view, right intention, right action, right speech, right livelihood, right effort, right mindfulness, and right concentration. Mary Weddell used the meaning of the Eightfold Path to express the balanced method of spiritual development through color and sound, by "breaking old molds" facilitated through continuing nightly visits to the heavenly Planes, through awareness, prayer, meditation and other spiritual tools.

LIONS We call the stumbling blocks on the Eightfold Path of development "lions on the path" or "lions along the way." The lion was the insignia of old Egypt and appears symbolically in all religions. We liken our undesirable faults to lions. A large part of our work on the Planes is to confront these lions and subdue them, overcoming negative traits that hinder progress.

DEVELOPMENT Development involves gaining wisdom and knowledge, becoming more compassionate and loving, and attaining spiritual gifts. Development through Color also brings attention to the progression of spiritual talents, the reading of auras, spiritual hearing and seeing with the spiritual eyes. Some describe it as receiving the gifts of the Holy Spirit.

MAPS / CHARTS Included in the Planes of Heaven books are unique charts of heavenly realms that cite more than one hundred locations in Heaven. The maps depict areas of consciousness beyond materiality, and are used to help us make a connection between the visible and invisible worlds, guideposts for understanding of what lies beyond our lives on Earth. Thinking of these charts as illustrating states of consciousness, vibratory rates, and dimensions of being helps give us a more accurate picture of the Planes. The current book features maps of heavenly locations on the Plateau between the 8th and 9th Planes and on the 9th Plane visited by our class.

How does the foregoing apply to seekers today? How can readers adapt 9th Plane teachings to their own spiritual development? Our group was extraordinarily fortunate to have a living teacher in Mary Weddell, but those without an Earth teacher, reading on, will see that they too can visit the Planes of Heaven for spiritual development. After each section or chapter in this book, a background review will appear that should be helpful to both first time readers and those who have read some or all of the previous books in the Planes series, as well as to Mary's surviving students.

In *Here and Hereafter, Forever After*, Mary's 9th Plane teaching continues her interpretive approach to the Eightfold Path, begun in the previous book of the Planes series, *The Eightfold Path and the 8th Plane of Heaven*. Following this Path, our attempt to change patterns of thought and behavior is accelerated as we undergo stepped up training in learning to overcome self and circumstances. "Climbing" upward in the Planes to bring inner life into manifestation in the outer, our close knit group of several dozen spiritually interconnected minds focuses on reaching the next level in an ongoing search for enlightenment. As in previous Planes of Heaven books, portions of the chapters in this volume are frequently expressed in Symposium format. Additionally, Mary and her senior teacher Miriam B. Willis answer questions posed by class members.

The Planes of Heaven books are based on transcripts, recordings, and my own personal notes contained in notebooks I kept during the many years I attended classes.

*****

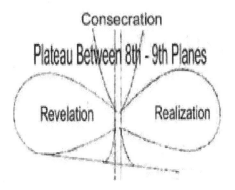

Area of Dimension of Consciousness

Area of Creative Energy and Power

Temple of Spiritual Responsibility

Area of Preparation for Divine Progression

PLATEAU BETWEEN THE 8TH AND 9TH PLANES

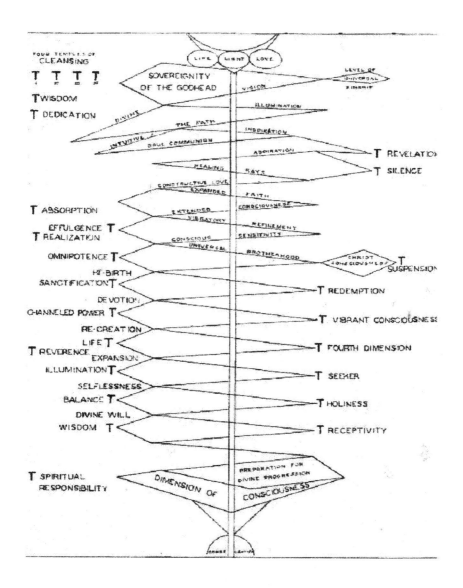

THE NINTH PLANE OF HEAVEN

JEANNE REJAUNIER

PART I

The Plateau

Review I

The 9th Plane

Review II

THE PLATEAU BETWEEN THE 8TH AND 9TH PLANES

What is a Plateau? What's the difference between a Plateau and a Plane?

Plateaus are areas located between heavenly planes. Their purpose is to review what we've learned on the previous plane and to prepare for the next plane. Along the lighted path of spiritual development, there is continuity from one plane to another, each with a plateau of review that contains the summing up of the qualities of the previous plane, much like final exams. On plateaus, we are tested on the qualities we developed on the plane just completed, and how we have absorbed and integrated what we learned. Every one of us must overcome to gain development. Each test must have built into the stature of the soul the degree of refinement needed for that level of development. We are continually tested and challenged to be sure we can walk the path.

Having completed our work on the 8th Plane, we enter the Plateau between the 8th and 9th Planes that is shaped like a clover leaf, stem down. Here we find areas and temples, including the Areas of Dimension of Consciousness, Creative Energy and Power, Preparation for Divine Progression, and Consecration; and the Temples of Spiritual Responsibility, Revelation and Realization.

AREA OF DIMENSION OF CONSCIOUSNESS

The Area of Dimension of Consciousness reveals the degree of balanced spiritual development one has attained. The seeker learns more of the faculties and powers to be used to progress on the Path, which in truth he has become. This realization stimulates ardent desire, for which he seeks guidance.

AREA OF CREATIVE ENERGY AND POWER

We're led to the Area of Creative Energy and Power, the reality and truth that "of myself alone. I can do nothing." In this vast, irregular diamond-shaped area, one sees the balance and imbalance of his consciousness, and through this illumination, is enabled to evaluate his needs. He reviews the many opportunities life has offered which he has let to slip past, unnoticed and unfulfilled. Once again he faces the question of why he reincarnated into the Earth school, and what is the primary purpose of life.

He understands more fully now that man is endowed with two fundamental attributes: consciousness and will; that consciousness is passive, will active; that consciousness is negative, will positive; that consciousness is acted upon, while will acts; that consciousness receives and will gives; that consciousness is a faculty and will is power. These are the working tools with which each of us builds our own individual temple of human character to attain soul maturity.

TEMPLE OF SPIRITUAL RESPONSIBILITY

"Behold, I have set before thee an open door " -- Holy Bible, Revelation 3:8

The parallel to the left side of the 9th Plane chart included with this book is the Temple of Spiritual Responsibility. This temple in the area at the bottom left on the chart is described as resembling a beehive of alabaster-like construction comprised of rope-like spirals of stone. Exceedingly strong, it is colored in the muted tones of the grey lavender spiritual ray of the holding force of patience and the soft fawn/ light biscuit color of steadfastness, in alternating stripes.

With others of like desire, the seeker is climbing a rugged path that requires focused attention, for there are attractive side paths into which one might wander. Resisting these, the seeker finds himself on a mesa of high ground covered with grass, while beneath his feet and stretching out before him is a path of his keynote color. This he follows in renewed faith, and is led to the Temple of Spiritual Responsibility.

The wind has changed. Breasting a fresh, clean breeze, the seeker presses forward. Invigorating strength fills his whole being. The temple looms before his eyes. It has a large central dome with spirals fashioned of rainbow colors, and is surrounded by many smaller domes. He is lifted toward the forecourt of the temple.

Our goal is the training of the spiritual mind, reconditioning thought patterns, clearing the subconscious. But we react to the bitter and to the sweet; we lack decisiveness. As we face ourselves, we wish to rise to spiritual responsibility. For this, we need unflagging faith, humility, and renewed consciousness. We bathe ourselves in the bright blue color of the 3rd ray of the Spiritual Arc of Blue. Its meaning: "Active realization of good, taking a positive stand, conscious awareness of talents and source of power."

AREA OF PREPARATION
FOR DIVINE PROGRESSION

Visiting the Area of Preparation for Divine Progression has earned the seeker sufficient power and enabling grace to ascend. Silent and yielding, he and many others advance over a green sward of velvety grass.

He sees a massive building with a long colonnade of pillars arched high, supporting a lotus petalled dome of translucent alabaster, shimmering with light in opalescent blue, with the palest yellow of illumination together with delicate rose and lavender, magnificent in a shower of softly swirling light. The pillars are of pale green onyx, the floor of rose quartz crystal. On each side of this colonnade are doors between the pillars.

The seeker is led along the colonnade until a door opens to the right or the left, where he instinctively knows he should enter. He finds himself utterly alone in a very small room. There is nothing in the room but a silken couch. On this he is glad to recline, for a great feeling of relaxation has come over him, as though everything from outside has receded. This experience is attended by a natural fear of the unknown and a longing to know the meaning and goal of this experience.

Faith is the only support he has, and as he uses this, he begins to penetrate his deepest motives and to realize the measure of his attainment and his need to triumph from the inner core to the outer expression in fulfillment.

He sees that functioning from within in purity of purpose is essential to living in the rhythm of sympathetic understanding. Compassion and selflessness must motivate his living if he is to progress in the balancing of forces toward divine adjustment. He knows he has attained powers that will operate through him in his perseverance.

TEMPLE OF REVELATION

VIOLET STEVENS This temple is one of stupendous and breathtaking grandeur. Entering through an open door, we find rows upon rows of individuals seated in an ever expanding circle. The center, a twenty foot space, is occupied by a great teacher. We notice that the floor is of pure crystal, diamond in shape, and reflects lights and colors with sparkling brilliance. The great teacher welcomes each of us by name, saying, "You earned this privilege by overcoming doubt and being loyal to the Path. There is much work to be done, work that is varied according to your needs."

Two colors radiate in my being: the 8th and 9th Rays of the Spiritual Arc of Purple. The 8th Ray, harmony, is a soft grayed pink lavender. The stabilizing force of grey, the controlling vibration of blue and warming energy of pink merge to provide harmony in a wholeness of many parts. Harmony gives us the power to be in the love rhythm of the universe. The 9th Ray of the Spiritual Arc of Purple, rose peach, is the color of gratitude.

We all feel the love of assembled seekers pouring out, as the hearts of the many blend as one. Music vibrates to a song that is developing in every soul, only more glorious, more triumphant, and more divine. It is a vibration of power so alive, so glorified it's felt from one's depth of being. All is color and light, the light of almighty God flowing out from the very center of eternity to create, redeem and make alive our own song of life. I call my song the song of gratitude, for as it pours into my being in complete fullness, I realize the purpose and the power of infinite harmony.

This is the new song not learned in words, but released from the very center of the soul, known as the celestial symphony of the universe, the Channel's gift to a developed person. When this precious melody of love becomes the living essence of one's being, its power begins to manifest. It is for all mankind to express. The song contains the power for man to forget himself and live in a new world, as man can live in peace and beauty as he walks the Eightfold Path, the great path of immortality now, one world without end, amen.

MARY When the heavenly teacher asks us a question, you first think you can't answer to save your life, but all of a sudden you can, because your soul is prompting you with the answer. We're holding up empty cups, and they're being filled from the Most High, because we've gone devotedly to these temples. We're not just "us" when we're there; we're in our spiritual bodies, and our souls are exposed to the light of understanding. The teachers expect us to be able to take the tests, and by example show other people in our lives how to live. That's one of the great things the temples are for, and it's a remarkable thing.

TEMPLE OF REALIZATION

This temple of beautiful design is surrounded by exotic foliage and exquisite flowers that enhance the intent of the temple. The beauty and fragrance of the flowers emphasize flowering spiritual precepts within for our edification and appreciation. We're given insight to the temple's teachings. These truths are set forth: recalling past favors; perceiving truth; awareness of our obligations; and eradicating disharmony. "Love the Lord thy God with all thy heart and mind and love thy neighbor as thyself."

A keynote of this temple's teaching was sounded in the word "adventure." This holds for us a challenge whereby we resolve to build a citadel activated by spirit, soaring to new heights, which paves the way to clarity of purpose and opens up new horizons. An interwoven pattern of integration received in the soul's sojourns at night together with practice revealed in daily living matures the ego. Keeping in balance in our daily living is of high importance. The growth we realize in this temple is cleansing and stabilizing, yet we know that discipline is ever required to develop further the inner powers of the conscious mind.

MARY Many realizations become awareness in the Temple of Realization. One gathers here a most beautiful and satisfying bouquet of spiritual flowers whose fragrance has permeated every area of thought and consciousness. Each flower has been carefully nurtured, its message absorbed in the perfection of fullness. Life has been unified in the rhythm of harmonic qualities. One's soul is filled with joy and gratitude for so many gifts. Love is the great invisible pattern of God's creation, the never-ending answer to all the question marks in man's consciousness from the simplest to the most profound.

MARGARET BRANCHFLOWER In the Temple of Realization, I was aware of several beautiful and stirring colors, in particular: the 7th Ray of the Psychological Arc of Red – pink rose lightly underlaid with pale orange, meaning love; the 8th Ray of the Psychological Arc of Red – light salmon pink, meaning joy; and the rose peach color of gratitude, which the 9th Ray of the Spiritual Arc of Purple.

AREA OF CONSECRATION

JEANNE REJAUNIER I had a profound experience on the Other Side one night this week. I was walking with a guide along a straight – perhaps half a mile long – path about ten feet wide with tall foliage on both sides. Dense trees shaded us and made everything look darker than usual. I wished I could have ridden this path on horseback rather than having to walk it, which means I probably would have liked to take an easier road, or have someone else (a horse) assume responsibility for carrying me over it. But I had to walk every step of this path myself.

The interesting thing about the trees was that they continually emitted psychological and spiritual colors to alert me what I needed to pay attention to, what I need to overcome, and/or things I thought I was free of that could easily crop up again, so that I should be sure to recognize them. It seemed like a very long time the guide and I were walking together, during which these color rays kept appearing. Each one would swirl around in the atmosphere, then dissipate and vanish. I saw five color rays in this manner. Four of the rays were from Psychological Arcs and one from a Spiritual Arc. These are:

The 1st Ray of the Psychological Arc of Yellow - orange streaked with dark brown and dark green, the color of deceit;

The 2nd Ray of the Psychological Arc of Blue - ashen grey-blue, meaning fear;

The 3rd Ray of the Psychological Arc of Yellow - medium yellow gray-green, with a yellow ochre midray dirtied with gray-green, meaning cowardice;

The 5th Ray of the Psychological Arc of Red - grayed olive green with a dirty orange midray, the color of greed;

The 2nd Ray of the Spiritual Arc of Green - dark olive green with a dark orange/henna midray, meaning self centeredness and stubbornness.

Finally, my guide and I came to the end of the long shaded path and out into the open. We were on a mountaintop with a thrilling grand vista that lay in front of us. I beheld the wide expanse of a golden road made of some crumbly material that seemed like soft golden nuggets. I know of no earth material that looks like this, but the gold of this road was so beautiful, wide and wide-reaching.

The road appeared to be composed of two rays of the Spiritual Arc of Yellow, the 4th and 11th rays, the colors of canary yellow and rich sun yellow, respectively.

My guide led me to a building with fully transparent walls, so it didn't seem like we were inside a building at all. Inside were placed several – I'm not sure what they're called, but it's the type of mini-telescope thing you see on mountain lookouts where tourists can gaze into and see at a long distance. Even though I examined about six or eight of these, I don't recall what I saw in any of them.

The next part of the experience I do recall, going out once more to survey that amazing golden road, looking over the horizon at a land that was like a promising new world, almost another country, that could be entered by walking only a few more miles into it. I heard the guide say something about "Pakistan," as if this country might be Pakistan. I've been to Pakistan, and nothing I saw in my travels there resembled this golden road, so maybe the word became corrupted in my mind in transference from heavenly to earth consciousness. Perhaps the word "Pak" means "to pack," signifying preparing for a spiritual journey? Maybe the word "stan" means "to stand," as taking a positive stand.

I want to say that I was overwhelmed by this experience, because it was one of the deepest and most meaningful ever of my night work. Words don't begin to do justice to the impact of this incredible experience.

MARY We've said before how hard it is to manufacture words to accurately describe these heavenly experiences, and how they affect us so remarkably.

ESTHER ESTABROOK Where on the Plateau did Jeanne's experience occur?

MARY We've come to the end of the Area of Consecration at the top of the Plateau between the 8th and 9th Planes, ready to begin our journey into the 9th Plane. What Jeanne described is looking out from the Area of Consecration on the Plateau to the beginning of our destination of the 9th Plane.

MIRIAM WILLIS Shall we talk about the positive and inspiring colors Jeanne saw on that golden road?

MARGARET Jeanne saw two colors from the Spiritual Arc of Yellow, the 4th and 11th Rays. The 4th Ray, the color of canary yellow, means "life consciously identified with spiritual principles; endeavoring to keep integrated by Spirit." The inflow of spiritual light available with this ray feeds the inner being, so that intuition increases and mental processes are sharpened.

ESTHER BARNES The 11th Ray of the Spiritual Arc of Yellow, a rich sun yellow, is sometimes known as "the Christ ray," and describes the maturing process. It's a ray that feeds and stimulates spiritual growth.

VIOLET Jeanne said she thought the word "stand" could mean "standing," as when we stand in the royal purple of faith, a reminder of the faith that's constantly needed along the Path. The 3rd Ray of the Spiritual Arc of Blue, which Jeanne mentioned, a bright blue color, means "taking a positive stand."

ESTHER BARNES Another "standing" ray is the 1st Ray of the Spiritual Arc of Green, a dark green and gray-brown color with an orange streak at its left side. This is the color at the base of the aura in which all human beings stand. It reaches beneath the feet, and without it, we would lack grounding.

MIRIAM WILLIS "I will pour out my spirit upon all flesh," saith the Lord. "The earth is white unto the harvest." We hear these words in that Area of Consecration.

******

REVIEW I
WHAT ARE THE PLANES OF HEAVEN?

The Planes of Heaven is our spiritual point of origin, the place where we "lived" before incarnating in this Earth life, and it is our destination after we pass from life on Earth. We come from the Planes, we continue after death on the Planes. To prepare for our future journey as well as to enrich us in the present, we may visit the Planes in sleep every night of our lives here on Earth.

The Planes of Heaven are expressions of the soul's growth and progression. They represent levels, dimensions, different states and conditions through which an individual soul passes along the way of spiritual ongoing, the inner reality awaiting all who wish to know the meaning and purpose of life here and hereafter. In our deepest understanding, we may become aware of the existence of these different realms, each of which is in one sense a world in itself, though in the wider sense, all are parts of one magnificent whole. They are definite and distinct evolutionary steps to which we ascend in our progressive unfoldment.

We are living in two worlds simultaneously, the visible and the invisible. Together, these two separate yet irreparably linked domains comprise the essence of "living in immortality now." It is one world without end, amen, as Mary always said, and the so-called "otherworld" is as close as our hands and feet. We are one in consciousness, if we so desire.

The study of the Planes of Heaven is an opportunity to get in touch with the sacred inner life and to nourish the soul. The link between this life and the afterlife becomes stronger as you progress in the Planes.

******

THE 9TH PLANE

MIRIAM WILLIS As we begin our journey to the 9th Plane of Heaven, let us consider the mystery, the reality, and the blindness to our conscious mind of that which happens to us in sleep. We've wondered about it. Then there came a day when, through seeking, searching, trusting, we began to realize that something great and wonderful occurred during that time of rest and refreshment. Continuing to search within the confines of our being, we discover treasures of this mysterious refreshment, this wonderful renewal: beautiful visions, dreams, remembrances and mysteries. These ephemeral things as they come to us intermittently in various ways, these touches of reality, cause us to go ever seeking to know more, to understand and to become.

The soul takes flight in sleep. How do we know this? We verify it by signs of growth in our understanding and in our soul's stature. As we turn to prayer and meditation, and through this, the uplift of our conscious mind, we fan that flame into a greater light.

What causes us to search, to seek? Is it not desire? Cries of the soul and the mind, the need ever to know more, to reach higher, to become greater? Yet there's a difference, a difference in the kind of growth we experience. For with this additive, there comes humility, love, and self forgetfulness in a concern for others. This is the reward of every seeker. It's been your reward and mine many times.

And still the treasure of that which is greater lures us on, for the soul of man desires to know. Step by step we rise upon the love that has been built within us, above the wisdom that attends it, the faith that guards it, and the eagerness that causes us to search. Let us go on searching to bring the hidden wholly to our mind, to rest in faith and confidence that when that flame within has furnished enough light and strength, we shall truly know.

Let us take a moment and consciously fan with the holy breath of the divine life, that flame within, and see it in our imagination becoming greater radiance, more beautiful in color, more selfless in desire. Let us note the color of these jewels; let us apply their meaning and rely on the strength they bring.

On the 8th Plane, we began the work of the Eightfold Path, receiving training in setting aside the smaller self, expanding discipline in overcoming self and circumstances. The 9th Plane brings to greater maturity the qualities of the Eightfold Path, manifesting more the inner life in the outer. Thus is there greater expression of the Eightfold Path goals of "right view, right intention, right action, right speech, right livelihood, right effort, right mindfulness, and right concentration," results of the heavenly experience of growth brought back to Earth.

Wondrous visions are given the seeker on his 9th Plane journey. As he opens his eyes after a deep silence to a sudden revelation, the seeker is initially spellbound. Then as divine life begins to flow in his veins once more, he recognizes that a complete change is taking place in him. The uplift we experience fills us with awe and an impetus to be faithful in all areas of living. Here many rhythmic laws are built into our being, enabling us to live more joyously and to function on the 9th Plane level of consciousness in our Earth lives.

The 9th Plane is a ladder of diagonal powerlines up which the seeker climbs. These diagonal powerlines are called "The Steeps of Heaven." They are the passageway on which we travel in our nightly sojourns to the Planes, going from right to left, backwards and forwards. Each Steep covers a large area containing six stations of testing, cleansing, learning, and power building. At the apex of each Steep are temples and other large areas for our ongoing.

The Stations on the Steeps represent something beyond what words can express. As we get out of the mind to go deeper, higher, and listen in the silence for expanded meaning, we see clearly the need to change and grow into qualities of spiritual progression. At the Stations of each Steep we face, shed or embrace positive and negative aspects and qualities of our lives, such as humility, selflessness, compassion, compatibility, justice, as well as pride, selfishness, hostility, and a seemingly endless list of "lions" – negative dispositional traits we need to overcome. We need to plumb the depths of our subconscious for this purpose.

MARY We become especially aware that our standard of life and motives eventually have to be "single," as "thine eye be single." How often do we find it hard to treat everybody with the same kind of love and compassion, to feel the inner fullness that encompasses the singleness of purpose we're ideally seeking? In these temples and on these steeps, all that we are is tested and needs to pass the level of development where we find ourselves.

******

REVIEW II
NIGHTTIME SOUL TRAVEL

When we sleep, we all "go" somewhere, whether to the Planes of Heaven or to the Sleep World, the latter, as mentioned in the Bible, being a rest area for souls who are not in spiritual work on the

Planes. In the Sleep World, the soul may experience dreams that, filtered to the intelligence of the dreamer, can awaken his deepest subconscious, causing him to desire spiritual advancement and to visit the Planes. If he lacks an Earth teacher, he will be taken there in his sleep by a heavenly guide.

Before we as seekers can expect enhanced consciousness, we need to create chemical changes in the spiritual body, to partake of the new atomic essence that entering the higher life requires. We do this through training and self examination on the Other Side. This means of spiritual development both prepares us for our future journey in the Afterlife, and enriches our lives in the present.

Travel in sleep to the heavenly realms is a part of the inner knowledge of all faiths, and has been practiced throughout the ages for more than ten thousand years of recorded history. The Bible speaks of the Planes. Hindus, Buddhists, Tibetans, Persians, Egyptians, Native Americans, ancient Hebrews, Greeks, Essenes, and early Christians all avowed the reality of communication between the visible and invisible worlds, recognizing that when human consciousness is focused on the inner planes in sleep, the liberated soul is free to commune with its own nature and to partake of the energies of the world beyond.

Leaving the physical body in sleep, the spiritual or soul body "goes out," ascending to the invisible world for ongoing development. Here, we examine and evaluate our lives. We receive guidance, healing and initiations, face self-correction, and clear the subconscious of accumulated negativity. We're imparted with heightened spiritual energy that carries over into our daily lives on Earth. We're tested over and over in tests which are later paralleled in the physical world. The activities we experience in the heavenly realms are geared to our own individual level of understanding, with the goal of increasing that understanding so that we become more fully developed people.

During nights on the Other Side, we're being taught to live in the spiritual body for short periods of time. When this life is over and we step into the next world to inhabit that other dimension of reality, our consciousness will go with us to the extent that we have developed it in our Earth lives. Thus do we live in two worlds at the same time: visible and invisible – indivisible. Thus do we store our treasure in Heaven and prepare our future home for the transition of life after life – a "death" which is not an extinction, but a welcoming into the fullness of eternity.

And the purpose of all the planes is evolution of the spirit.

******

PART II

STEEPS AND STATIONS OF THE STEEPS

OTHER 9TH PLANE TEMPLES

REVIEWS III - XV

Filled with the strength of creative power, we begin our climb along the FIRST STEEP of the 9th Plane and its Six Stations of Learning. We are tested along each station in this progression.

> First Station: SERVICE. Service answers the call of love, no matter how the call is received. 9th Plane service is grateful, and often secretly given.
>
> Second Station: SILENCE. The key to effective self-knowledge and growth. Through Silence the great Voice is heard and answered.
>
> Third Station: MEDITATION. Communion in love with the infinite giver of all.
>
> Fourth Station: PRAYER. A state of soul, being at one with the heavenly realm, with a purpose, whether stated or not. Through prayer, one's aid to others is strengthened, purified, ennobled and heartened by added power from the invisibles.
>
> Fifth Station: POWER. This station enables one to bring forth spiritual gifts latent within.
>
> Sixth Station: AT-ONE-MENT. This is the station wherein all is clearly seen and understood, bringing to Earth moments of one pointed clarity. It includes at-one-ment, reforming into balance immature or warped conditions of being.

******

THE TEMPLE OF RECEPTIVITY

VIOLET Having experienced on the Plateau the Preparation for Divine Progression and having expanded consciousness and deepened understanding, we're ready for training in the Temple of Receptivity. We've come to the place where we so desire to face every obstacle standing in the way of our advancement that we'll gladly enter into the fuller training we need. No more glossing over a fault, no shirking the revelation of a lack, no more putting aside inevitable testings, but entering into them with full free will, truly wanting the necessary cleansing. In full accord and in joyous expectation, we're ready for the next step forward, no matter what shall be revealed; we're ready to receive, come what may. In triumphant readiness we view the Temple of Receptivity.

It embodies a state of soul expectation, for it is a stately temple. Its lines are dignified yet solid. It is reminiscent of an Egyptian temple, Karnack in particular. We enter a great hall, its roof upheld by magnificently tall, sandstone pillars in the lotus bud design. The solidity of the columns is symbolic of God's unchanging laws, and we have tested ourselves against these laws.

Between the pillars a guide awaits. We ask him how to proceed. He directs us to a certain spot along the wall where we enter a door leading into a small chamber. We enter a power filled atmosphere. We're alone with our thoughts. These soon bring to mind things done or left undone that seemed insignificant at the time, but which now loom large in our consciousness. As we reflect on particular experiences, the clearer our lesson becomes.

As the stark reality of our laziness, lack of sympathy, and indifference are revealed, we are shown the magnitude of the effect. The color of indifference, the 1st Ray of the Psychological Arc of Green, is murky green with a clouded apricot midray, a combination that reveals insensitivity, disinterest and apathy.

All details are uncovered until they seem as though squeezed out as one squeezes water out of a sponge, and truly one feels like a sponge after experiencing this form of testing. If a deed was done in loving desire to be of service, then the review we receive discloses all aspects of such a revelation, and we realize the beauty of service, what it requires and what it accomplishes. These tests continue until all is cleared out and we feel ready to advance.

MIRIAM WILLIS The Temple of Receptivity is the first temple on the 9th Plane. Find it on the right side of your chart. In our progression up the Planes, we've encountered other Temples of

Receptivity, each being a higher octave of the previous one. Its very name rouses in the heart of the seeker a desire to open the inner chambers of his being to enlightened guidance of the development he has already received, and to discover the depths and heights of his motives and aspirations.

Two things stand out at this point. First, the massiveness and splendor of this temple. The huge edifice is supported by pale green onyx pillars lifting high into a canopy of lotus like leaves that looks down upon a floor scintillating with rose quartz. This, in short, is the outer adornment of the temple that houses sacred truths.

Second, there is an initial feeling of unworthiness as we approach the teachings, teachings that seem like unto a star casting light upon the soul of man. Breathless, we come face to face with reality. Are we ready for the searchlight of testing revealing our preparation, our inadequacies and our present development? Overcoming faults is always our first consideration, for faults deter, delaying spiritual progress. We examine ourselves, only to find that first things first have not always been too well followed.

There is hope through patience. Stop, look, listen, wait for a signal, then go forth under the sanction of your soul. Pray. Prayer is food for the inner man. It has power to overcome; it is ointment as well as direction. Prayer is a door opener. When we've first screened out the self, we have a clear consciousness, for the light from above unhampered shines through, and "he doeth the works."

We give thanks: for our faithful teachers, our daily communions, our heritage, for good health, for our highest hope, for our faith, for more than we can mention. There are many who haven't tasted the above blessings. May we share some of this bounty.

All the treasures we find in the Temple of Receptivity, both good and regrettable things, are found in the deep well of our being, not only revealed in the mirrors of revelation but within the very deepest caverns of our own selves. We're thankful for the glimpses of recognition that filter through to us. We pray that we may lay hold upon them, recognize them and give them the impetus and attention that will cause them to grow. And so, we lift it in this blessed power, we rest all that we are, all that we have, and know that the goodness of truths will filter through to transform us, so that as we touch the hem of his garment, we lay hold to eternal life.

MARY We enter this Temple of Receptivity with the normal feeling of anxiety which we face on the threshold of any new adventure. If only we could have a guarantee that our present hopes would never betray us, leaving us deserted in a lonely place, then we would find the peace we long for. But life isn't like that. The future is never quite a thing apart from all that's gone before. We bring into the present ingredients and cargoes from the past that are with us as we take the untrod path. All we've learned, felt and thought, all our experiences from birth to now, all the love that nourished us, all the yearning rooted in our spirits are with us as we move into the unknown way.

The seeker experiences an abiding desire to know the future, to see around the corner of the days and years. Even when he believes what will happen next month or next year doesn't concern him, the insistence still remains; the seeker wants to know. We see that a shadow often falls between man and his vision. We know the gulf that lies between the goal or dream and its fulfillment is wide and deep. We recall Christ's words as we come out of sleep, "To him who waits, all things reveal themselves, provided he has the courage not to deny in the darkness what he has seen in the light."

For some, waiting is a time of intense preparation for the next leg of the journey. Here at last comes a moment when a new attack upon an old problem can be set in order. Or it may be a time of soul searching, checking past failures against present insight. It may be a moment of the long look ahead when the landscape stretches far in many directions, and the chance to select one's way among several choices can't be hurried. For some seekers, waiting is more than this.

In this zone of becoming where balance is gained following instructions received in the Temple of Receptivity, we're developing creative power and forming a pattern of recollection in which is called into focus the fragmentary values we've held, until we have to reckon with life's reality. We watch the gathering darkness until all light is swallowed up completely, without the power to interfere or bring a halt.

To continue the journey in darkness, with our footsteps guided by the illumination of remembered radiance gives us courage to know our soul is in the lead and that it sings the song of truth, the song of the 9th Plane. The spirit sings within like some winged creature from above. Light is all around. The sky is lost in light; we know the might of God's unceasing love. Waiting, waiting, waiting ... we think of this time as a window opening on many landscapes.

Not by bread alone does man live, but by the dreams that can be spaced for inner things. Lost in the labyrinth of song and light, the hills pick up the words of love and give them sound all around and everywhere. "Man shall not live by bread alone."

LOLA GRUBE "The world is singing the song of 9th Plane." Is it a definite song, or ... ?

MARY It's a song that remains with us. It means that the song of our life changes into a higher octave and rhythm, which makes us seek to develop more, especially to be more giving, loving and understanding.

PATTI CHALGRIN We experience many tests along each of the Steeps, and I suppose we go back when we fail and have to be retested? Does that mean going back to the 8th Plane?

MARY We may go even farther back. Because it has been a repeated thing from the earlier Plane, where we were supposed to be fortified through our development to be able to resist and correct. We have to be in tune with the 9th Plane to make progress. It's a very hard thing to get off that 9th Plane and to get onto the 10th. If you can learn the patience of waiting ...Patience and waiting are two great guideposts along the way of development.

I do believe that we bring with us a certain set of faults that appear over and over again in our lives. And perhaps, when we're able to look back into our past lives, we've seen those same mistakes that are following through. Perhaps that's the reason we've come back to Earth, to experience these things again and see how well we can work out our recovery from the pitfalls that seem ever to be before us.

We have an urge within us, which is why you're seeking. This urge was planted within you when you came into this world, that natural urge to seek God, to find the highest and the most for happiness. When one is attuned with spirit, the soul asks for more. If one becomes a seeker, he accepts the fact that his life is strictly between himself and God. The seeker has the innate wisdom and grace to accept life's pattern as traced upon his soul at birth. He realizes these patterns will be given him again through dreams, visions, and the revelations received in his night work in the Halls of Memory and in the Temples of Learning.

*****

REVIEW III
HOW DO WE GO TO THE OTHER SIDE AT NIGHT?

The Silver Cord: As we travel out of our bodies, the spiritual part of us is lifted above material forces, while the physical body remains inert. Our spiritual bodies are connected to our physical bodies by the spiritual cord, also known as the silver cord. This radiant cord, which is attenuated when traveling out of the body, is referred to in Scriptures (Ecclesiastes 12:6-7): "Or ever the silver cord be loosed ... then ... the spirit shall return unto God who gave it," and was known to exist from time immemorial.

The silver cord suspends us from Earth to Heaven. It remains attached throughout our nighttime experiences; it is not severed until the transition of death, our graduation from this Earth school.

In Mary's Color and Planes teaching, this silver cord that extends for night travel is named the "Sixth Ray of the Spiritual Arc of Yellow," called "Illumination." This ray is described as "....pale silvery blue/white with a pale yellow underlay ... a living ray ... radiant, permanent, seen in all auras ... It is like an etheric counterpart of the physical umbilical cord ... is the lifeline that guides the soul's return to the physical body in soul travel ... stretching as far as needed ... is severed only at death. When attenuated, it stretches as far as is needed for out of the body travel."

Method of Travel: The soul travels on the silver cord along Nature's Creative Energy to the Planes for spiritual night training. Taken in sprit by way of a powerline, we are aided by etheric lodestones. These lodestones raise our vibration, furnishing creative energy for us to move. The light of the lodestones lifts us as we go climbing through the Planes, carrying us along. As we travel through the spirit world, riding on the wide rail of light that is the powerline, we may feel those lodestones picking us up along our climbs through the heaven world.

Arrival in the Heaven World: We arrive at a landing field, a vast and beautiful area centrally located on the 3rd Plane, which Mary referred to euphemistically as "Grand Central Station," because so many groups of spiritual seekers from all corners of Earth assemble there.

We're in another realm now, and we're in the spirit body. Each person enters the rhythm according to the development of his soul. We alight at this "Grand Central Station" only briefly. Shortly after our initial landing, we're lifted to a separate destination for further ongoing. We're now on our way for training in the temples and halls of learning on the higher planes.

*****

> SECOND STEEP   To the AREA OF DIVINE WILL and the TEMPLE OF WISDOM.
>
> First Station: COMPASSION   Compassion is the artful act of looking deeply into a soul and seeing the God-center, a reaching in, as it were, and drawing forth inner calm that clears the troubled surface. Compassion is a deep love of soul for soul and the inner recognition of God in others.
>
> Second Station: SURRENDER. Handing the little self over to Spirit, that Spirit will guide and expand the small view.
>
> Third Station: CONTENTMENT. Letting go of the lesser view for the greater. Receiving with happy heart that which God has intended for us, while remaining in devoted service to him.
>
> Fourth Station: AWARENESS - knowing that something – a situation, condition, a problem – exists.
>
> Fifth Station: ADORATION - intense admiration culminating in reverence and worship.
>
> Sixth Station: JOY -   the emotion evoked by wellbeing, good fortune; delight, a state of happiness, felicity, bliss.

Leaving the Temple of Receptivity, one is filled with an effulgence seeking expression. The seeker's way unfolds to him through the six tests on the Steeps leading to the 9th Plane Area of Divine Will and the Temple of Wisdom.

HELEN von GEHR In an experience I recalled from one night, I was in my house. There was such a rain as I've never seen, and no matter where I went, the rain was beating down on the house. Would that be a water test?

MARY You nearly always get that as you go further into this 9th Plane. It's very cleansing. It takes out so many of our idiosyncrasies we've lived with that have heretofore been unrecognized. It often makes me think of being washed whiter than snow, because you feel as if you're dressed in a white garment when you come out.

We learn that the Path only becomes known as we fulfill certain conditions. By trial and error, as we continue the search, faith leads us to answers. We realize more deeply that faith and love need the selective force of wisdom. An urgent longing earns us entrance to the next area and temple.

TEMPLE OF WISDOM

MIRIAM WILLIS The Temple of Wisdom is tremendously vast. It reaches through many Planes and influences many conditions. We go back and forth to a number of the temples on the 9th Plane that you've already heard of in the lower planes. And now we've come to consider the experiences we had, each one a little different, in the Temple of Wisdom.

The Temple of Wisdom stands on a hill in blazing gold like the sun, so brilliant one can't see its form for the glory of it. The emanation of its shining casts rays of lighted paths through the forest of trees that lies between the seeker and his goal. As he follows one of these rays, the seeker comes into a clearing, and the form of the temple becomes increasingly distinct. He sees that it's similar to the spider web of the great Temple of Wisdom at the top of the 5th Plane.

He enters at the level of his development. As he progresses, there flashes through him a realization that he can only possess and apply wisdom up to this level. His longing for expansion, however, causes him to press on for further testing. He finds himself in a place of many mirrors that reflect exactly the actions and reactions of situations he has experienced in his Earth life. Because of the power of the wisdom in which he stands, he can now clearly see where and why he failed and how to improve similar situations in the future. This objective viewing so impresses him that it becomes a part of his consciousness, and he feels not only an uplift but a conviction that he will know how to apply this new wisdom to his life.

This kind of testing is granted many times in differing faculties and situations mirrored in this temple, until the faculty of understanding and discrimination manifest in wisdom's harmonious fulfillment. A realization of the vast supply available to those who seek sweeps over him, together with recognition of a need to seek this wisdom at all times through the mirrored well of deep receptivity within.

MARY We go to this great Temple of Wisdom as a revival of interest, to renew our faith, to be able to bring back to our daily living some vestige of what we've learned there. The teachers who speak in this temple are filled with desire that people of Earth follow development to where mankind can be lifted to believe more thoroughly that they can help bring peace to the world. I've heard many promises to mankind, if man could only live in peace. I don't doubt these promises; they're intended for man on Earth to experience. But man has first to learn that he must live with another, and that's the difficult thing. We read the history of past nations, knowing that today there are tribes that can't live in peace, who kill because of it. Do remember that the Master said, "As ye have done it to the least of you, ye have done it unto me."

ALMA JOHNSON I felt my experience in the Temple of Wisdom was extremely important to my innermost self. An essence remains with me, although details are elusive. I can't quite grasp them ... but I had a feeling of certainty about being led into a higher realm where I was given important guidance.

MARY It was a very beautiful and fulfilling time, and there weren't any of you who didn't feel absolutely greater for having been there. This Temple of Wisdom is a part of the Temple of the Living God. Faith is the cornerstone; above its lighted portals is the intuitive conviction of that which both reason and conscience approve. Please accept this truth and know that your spiritual body is an achievement of beautiful harmony, a living example of Christ's shining substance. Color guides the seeker through the hidden channels of darkness to the light.

VIOLET We spent seven nights in testing in the Temple of

Wisdom.

MIRIAM WILLIS The Life Ray surrounding all seekers is vitality of the future poured into the well of knowledge, to be drawn upon when the need arises. It's not the mental processes a developed one uses, but the voice and wisdom and words from this hidden spiritual source. Through the listening heart, we're told it's the nature of the universe to give us what we're able to take. There comes to each seeker the logical and exact result of his own receptivity. To each, life brings the reward of his own thinking and visioning.

MARY Music that had been developing in each one's soul, only more glorious, more triumphant, more divine, to create, redeem, and make alive, became a vibration of power that was flowing around us in light and colors from the very bosom of eternity. When this precious melody of love becomes the living essence for all mankind to express. Our song of life is the Channel's gift to a developed person. The keynote contains the song, the song contains the power for man to forget himself and know he lives in one world without end.

*****

AREA OF DIVINE WILL

MIRIAM WILLIS The privilege of many reviews is granted to the earnest seeker as he climbs the heavenly Steeps of the lighted path of spiritual progression. It doesn't surprise us that we have to visit the Area of Divine Will many times when we consider what's involved. I think you'll realize why we have to go here so often.

LOLA GRUBE After waking from being in the Area of Divine Will, I realized more deeply than ever, "Thy faith hath made thee whole." And I was thinking that in the Temple of Wisdom, we considered the miracle of living in belief and faith, and about the difference between belief and faith. I wonder if you would speak about that, Mary.

MARY There's a distinction between belief and faith. A man's belief is what he does, what he practices. There's nothing accidental or incidental about beliefs. They determine and are determined by the set of a man's spirit. This is a strange paradox. Out of the deep places of a man's heart flow the issues by which he lives. These issues are qualified by the things he does with consistency. On the other hand, faith has an element that seems to have no beginning and no end. It doesn't spring from sources that are under the control of the individual.

Faith gathers in as it sweeps the life, informing it with overtones of hopeful anticipations of the future. Faith envelops life and charges it with an energy that sustains and holds. It's the breath of God that becomes in all living things the breath of life. In the miracle of living in faith, man is at one with spiritual development.

We make a clear distinction between belief and faith because, generally speaking, belief has come to mean a state of mind which is almost the opposite of faith. Belief is the insistence that the truth is what one would wish it to be. The believer opens his mind to truth on the condition that it fits in with his preconceived ideas and wishes. Faith is an unreserved opening of the mind to whatever truth may turn out to be. Faith has no preconceptions; it is a plunge into the unknown. Belief clings, but faith lets go.

You can only know God through an open mind and heart. This is the point where the spirit in man and the spirit of God blend into one creative illumination. This is the great miracle, as man the seeker makes his way into the vast regions of the inner planes of life. Man comes to know that the world of spirit has vast frontiers to be discovered. He becomes aware that man without God is a seed blowing in the wind. I never ask you to accept any of these things. But to be able to believe is truly a gift of God's creation.

Of course, it's my faith that God answers prayer. I believe in the answer to prayer. And I believe that belief leads to faith. The harmonies of life deal with faith: faith in things, faith in friends, faith in our work. Whatever we're doing – it's bringing faith and harmony to rest upon it.

There is within every man a guidance that is greater than he knows. And by an understanding faith – not just belief – but a firm faith, he can receive that guidance. If I'm aware, that is, meditative toward the message of the Planes of development that the energy is expressing in me, I'll soon learn when the message I'm receiving is of God versus when it's produced by my own identification systems.

Faith begets true belief that transcends commonplace belief, and lies in conviction. You don't just believe. You know.

MIRIAM WILLIS Notice that the key color of the 9th Plane, opaline blue, the 10th Ray of the Spiritual Arc of Blue, applies very much to this. One facet of its meaning is the ability to differentiate imagination from the real.

MARY The key word of this Area of Divine Will is "seeing." Man's development will be measured by his seeing awareness and by his capacity of sensing potential. Attention is the activity of will; awareness is a provision of intuition. These are the words that best describe the activity of the Area of Divine Will.

When I'm in the presence of a sunset, I'm aware of beauty. It's not just an intellectual experience, for my heart is telling me the energy and content of beauty. I'm feeling beauty; the energy is communicating itself to me.

ESTHER BARNES I wondered about something I saw. The 9th Plane major color keeps coming through to me, opalescent blue, the 10th Ray of the Spiritual Arc of Blue. I saw a pathway over which was a structure composed of intermingled hexagons that formed like a spider web. They were high up, and all were in the color of that opalescent blue, meaning "spiritual balance ... discernment between imagination and revelation of truth ... integration of spiritual powers" ... I'm trying to relate meaning to this vision I saw.

MIRIAM WILLIS Development of this ray enables one to tell the difference between truth and imagination. The ray helps one to interpret dreams and visions with deeper insight. I would think you're being blessed with a supply of the ray for this purpose.

BILL JACKSON   Excuse me, but I don't quite understand what "Divine Will" is.

MARY   To will, as I will to do something, is action. Divine Will also works in action, but in an abstract way. So will has to come from a source of supply that we don't have actively before us. Then the creative energy of God's love ties the two together. It's like tying stardust. It's something so beautiful when you really feel you're doing the will of the Father. In doing that, we've called forth within our natures all that harmonizes and abandoned all that displeases, that which we carry around with us as a mantle of guilt. Because after we once know we're working with divine force and feel the creative energy flow within us, everything is different.

MIRIAM WILLIS   Judgment becomes a pure ray of understanding, and after a while, there's a will to do the thing as it should be done, a will to see far enough and deep enough that we know we're going to change the things that are corrupting our thinking. And we've learned where the source of supply is that will change human lives.

MARY   There are so many tests we take every day; we learn how to sink into that Divine Will when we're in a hard spot.

MIRIAM ALBPLANALP   Such as facing a test of someone's anger, for instance.

MARY   "Go thou within and lift" – the words, the response, will be given you. Therefore, know that when Divine Will comes through and answers, you'll to do the right thing. I often think of Divine Will and the will of man as running along the wires, and I feel that both speak. Out of the darkness will come the inner voice that guides us, if we can put our own will back long enough to listen. And this listening attitude brings the answer. I say that through Divine Will, life can be changed.

Wholesome, holy respect leads to fulfillment of Divine Will. We're shocked at our failure to measure up to such a standard, and in humility we renew our faith with a depth of longing to dedicate our all to this concept. How wonderful every life would be if operated from this premise. No sacrifice would be too great if only life could be thus purified.

Listen for answers. Christ had them. Buddha got his answers. We can go right straight through our teachers and find that each one of them stopped long enough to listen to direction, and has followed divine will. And so, my thought to offer you is to live under divine right of understanding, the laws of willing ourselves to do, and being willing to expect answers.

The answers of the human body are very much in evidence when one is balanced. The vibratory activity of the mind and body increases if one can throw off the mantle of guilt and self-hatred, and withdraw their will under the plan that God has for them.

MIRIAM That's really quite a prayer, isn't it?

VIOLET Don't you think, Mary, often when you're following Divine Will, you have an inner happiness.

MARY Yes. Yes. Quite right, darling.

MIRIAM So true.

*****

REVIEW IV
TEMPLES AND HALLS OF LEARNING

The Planes of Heaven are populated by Temples and Halls of Learning where, guided by heavenly teachers, we are privileged examine and evaluate our lives and receive energy for growth and change. There are temples and halls of learning on every plane. In each one are different areas in which one's entire life is gone over both privately and with the heavenly guides. Another activity in the temples is visiting with loved ones who have preceded us to the Afterlife.

Our guides are evolved beings, many from the 100th and 200th Planes and beyond. They have "overcome the world," so to speak; their mission is helping others like us to advance.

Mirrors: As your life is examined in the temples, you see yourself through special mirrors. Some of these are called confession mirrors. We gaze into clear mirrors and black mirrors. The latter reveal your detriments, the former, your positive credits. These black mirrors look like black marble slabs. You wouldn't think there was anything there, but soon, before you know it, these areas of consciousness take on color, as written before your very eyes are things that you immediately realize should be corrected. The mirrors that we stand in front of are revealing ourselves to ourselves, the entire self.

You see yourself clearly, see mistakes you've been making and how you can change your life to reach the next level in spiritual growth. There are so many little hidden things in us, dark spots to be recognized and cleared out that crop up again and again. When we look into these mirrors, we see that we've brought a lot of faults with us needing our attention. We must overcome everything holding us back – guilt, fear, anger, criticism, resentment, selfishness; all our unwanted qualities, these memory patterns buried in the subconscious have to be faced and eliminated before we can progress. There is a day of reckoning, an accounting. We must be reconciled. Within that reconciliation, there is a deep respect for ourselves for what we have already overcome and accomplished.

Each temple contains examining rooms where one's life is gone over with the wise guidance of our heavenly teachers. Earth states of consciousness, particularly emotions, are revealed to us, exposed to a balancing process, cleansed and healed, and we're shown how to avoid past mistakes. As vibratory frequencies increase, these states and dimensions become less dense, increasingly refined and filled with more light. Eventually, realizations are brought to the consciousness of the seeker in the form of dreams and visions, insights and intuitions after the soul has returned to its body from which it has been attenuated by the silver cord.

No man is perfect while he lives upon this earth, but each man can improve until his enlightenment makes him aware of his faults and the falseness of his living.

Tests: In our night work in the higher realms, we're given tests to pass on the Stations of the Steeps and in the Temples. These tests are personal, functioning to meet the need of the individual. We have fire, water and air tests. Fire tests deal with physical purification; water tests purify the emotional body; and the mental body is cleared in air tests. The higher the plane, the more difficult and challenging the test.

These tests are a means of unfolding consciousness. There is specific testing and development in each steep and temple, and afterwards, there will always be a parallel test in the physical life to match.

*****

> THIRD STEEP To the TEMPLE OF HOLINESS
>
> First Station: PURITY This is a purifying station as well as a revealing one, where the Seeker checks his own attainments and motives in the bright, kindly light of Purity and sees what is needed to correct his aura.
>
> Second Station: SACRIFICE is giving up willingly and lovingly something one loves, needs or desires, for the benefit of another person or for a higher cause.
>
> Third Station: DEDICATION Selfless intention to be used as a channel for good, fully aware of the qualities of the 3rd Ray of the Spiritual Arc of Blue and the 12th Ray of the Spiritual Arc of Green.
>
> Fourth Station: FAITH is the bridge between the known and the unknown on any level. An outgoing faith in the essential rightness of all things.
>
> Fifth Station: CONSECRATION is to dedicate to God one's works (thoughts, talents, creations), the goal being to raise dedicated lives to consecrated living, through awareness of the Christ life more and more often each day.
>
> Sixth Station: HUMILITY is a loving, selfless, and patient waiting on the spiritual Voice; conscious of one's smallness as well as one's power.

******

MARY Feeling the need of purification, we gratefully enter the Station of Purity on the Third Steep of the 9th Plane. Here, in crystal clear fountains, we're cleansed again and again, each time the values of life becoming clearer. Through the process of purification, we become more unified, one-pointed Godward, able to rely on guidance within, and freed from selfish desire, frustration and conflict.

Thus, one is able to sincerely dedicate his life to high purpose, and is granted the privilege of entering the Station of Dedication, where we find rays of sapphire blue and amethyst penetrating our whole being, building the stability of perseverance needed to follow the dedicated way of life.

We are very aware of the bright blue 3rd ray of the Spiritual Arc of Blue, meaning "taking a positive stand, conscious awareness of source of power;" and of the delicate yellow green 12th ray of the Spiritual Arc of Green, meaning "at-one-ment with God, illumination, and a path clear through self control."

This requires much faith, and we're grateful to enter the Station of Faith for further infilling of faith's generous power. As its glorious royal purple rays envelop, we're renewed in confidence, discovering that as one acts in consecrated faith, one's powers increase.

This revelation causes us to feel a need for consecration, bringing us to the Station of Consecration. Here we enter a vale of periwinkle blue, which helps direct all motives toward unified purpose. On this Station we see life revealed as the garment of the great Creator manifesting love, wisdom and order. We see also the chaos caused by man's selfish use of his own free will. We discover that the ideal of living in the aura of consecration requires daily, hourly reliance on the power of divine rhythm.

We discovered a need to cultivate humility, which brings us to the Station of Humility, where we enter a ray of blue lavender overlaid with a mist of silver warmed with a touch of rose lavender. Bathed in this power, the revelation begins to unfold and the seeker sees that humility is neither shy nor forward; it contains the natural grace of respect for the opinions of others, giving them complete freedom even though we may not agree with their opinions. We can shine in the sun or bask in the shade with equal poise and freedom, and as we value our own free will, we pay equal tribute to that of our brother.

The powers of dedication, consecration, faith and humility stimulate memory and desire. Responsibility to be faithful in life's obligations is quickened and more constantly fulfilled.

THE TEMPLE OF HOLINESS

MIRIAM WILLIS The tests along the path toward the Temple of Holiness on the 9th Plane reveal the inner reality of creative action in a multitude of forms manifested through infinite intelligence, filling us with awe and reverence at the wonders unfolding within and around us. We're proud to be part of such order. We stand amazed at the infinite patience of the Creator. Even the ground beneath our feet is pulsing with life, and as we walk upon it, reverence fills our being.

In this consciousness we enter a mellow light. Crossing a delicate green bridge of desirelessness, we see a gleaming temple of circular loveliness in mother of pearl. Its iridescence seems to move as one becomes conscious of color and music issuing from it.

The carving about the great door is exquisite. We enter as through a silken veil. Inside, we find a great richness in depth and height of color. As so many very simple things are disclosed, in surprise and awe, we acknowledge the heart of everything we observe in a realization of the holiness of all life. Here we learn that all relationships can hold within them the essence of holiness, that holiness isn't a thing separate and apart, solemn and austere, but rather it's the reverent, happy appreciation of inner qualities that make life whole and holy.

Approaching the Temple of Holiness, we're greeted from the outside. The winged ones, those blessed angels, come forth and hover over us. The warmth and vibrant energy that enter our spiritual bodies we bring back in our human bodies when we return from our night work. This is evidence to many people of having been to the Temple of Holiness – through the vibrancy that seems to sing through our very muscles as we return to Earth. Yes, that's a real pattern, and you've seen it in this 9th Plane Temple of Holiness.

HELEN MARSH I saw one angel. . .and great radiance filled the whole heavens.

MARY That's a symbol as old as Old Egypt, a symbol of peace.

VIOLET We entered a great corridor of about twenty feet in width. The walls on either side were encrusted with diamonds. We were surrounded by glory and by hosts of angels. All the flashing lights of myriads of colors reflected and refracted and sparkled. One felt caught up in their brilliance. We drank of it as though being fed by power sent forth. One felt like a thirsty plant, parched, hungry for divine food. When it seemed we could take no more beauty, we moved forward and were led into a great spacious hall of vast proportions, coloring of which was in bands running the length of the audience hall.

At the base it was of a soft greyish lavender, a combination of the colors of humility and peace. Above that was the soft yellow color of illumination. Then came a sunrise effect which was topped by rainbow colors. I felt I was breathing the influence of divine order – becoming a part of creative energy. Through this experience I came into a deeper understanding of Color used as force of power operating in the whole of creation. In this glorious atmosphere each of us took on a portion of this power, absorbed it into his own being so that it became a precious possession.

As we proceeded, our eyes were focused like magnets on an altar at the far end. This was a force distinctly felt. I became conscious of soft music. As a whisper, it rose above all else, bringing its own message to us. This spoke to the heart, to the very inner core of our being, and gave the message each soul needed. The color surrounding the altar was that of the 10th Ray of the Spiritual Arc of Blue, opal iridescence. All seemed clear, real, and propelling of holy order.

MARY That's the Temple of Holiness, Violet, the left wing. There's a modern building that's been shown. Iridescent – has somewhat of a turquoise at the bottom of it, if you look closely the next time.

FRANK CRANDALL I saw something similar to what Violet brought through, and thought there were angels in the background, but I couldn't reach them.

JEANNE I had a water test last night in the Temple of Holiness. I remember being immersed in very refreshing water and emerging completely dry. The night before, I was in a walled garden where there were tulips around me.

MARY The Garden Beautiful.

MIRIAM WILLIS It's true that we aren't permitted to choose the path of desire, even though it might bring us farther into the Garden Beautiful. We wish so much to mingle with the angelic visitors who guide those seeking through the temples of learning. But we must wait our time.

EVA TOTAH What Jeanne said caused me to recall having been in a garden as well. I was with some Asian people, mother, father and children. I wondered why I was seeing Asians and what that could mean.

MARY Yes, dear. Well, you see, we're on the right side of the path going up, and the Temple of Holiness is for all nations, all creeds, all sects. All those that go up the Great Way go to those temples the same as we do.

JEANNE I remember two other places where I was. They were like covered silken passageways. One cover was turquoise, the 9th Ray of the Spiritual Arc of Blue – meaning truth of self attained, realization of growth. The other color was the royal purple of faith.

MARY That's the Temple of Holiness. That's good . Now keep track of those, will you? They'll be added to, very likely.

MIRIAM ALBPLANALP My vision started with symbol of a Caduceus in very pure white. The top had folded wings. Then the wings unfolded, and became what appeared to be doves. Then the dove forms turned into little angels. I could see the tiny faces and the folded wings open and in flight. In flight they had fiery red-gold and red halos. Powerful energy streamed all around. Then they began circling horizontally in a counterclockwise manner. As I woke up, I was given the words, "cherubims and seraphims." Seraphim in Hebrew means "the burning ones," angels, that is, and another reference called them "the fiery ones," and the cherubim were called "higher celestial beings."

VIOLET This brings to my mind the hymn "Holy, holy, holy - Lord God almighty ... cherubim and seraphim ... God in three persons, blessed Trinity." The hymn "Holy, holy, holy" is appropriate for the Temple of Holiness, is it not?

MIRIAM ALBPLANALP What I experienced was symbolic, but at the same time, there was that unmistakable understanding within of holiness, truth, reality, depth. Where did I see these cherubim and seraphim? In the Temple of Holiness, I believe.

MARY Well, we spoke, did we not, of the angelic hosts?

MIRIAM WILLIS One of the things we notice on the 9th Plane, Mary has said, is the increased presence of angels. We see them as never before, compared to the lower planes we've been to.

MARY In the Temple of Holiness we're told to have faith, not to doubt. Faith is the marriage of God and the soul, certainty of God's omnipotence through the soul, for with God all things are possible, because faith, as we have seen, really can move mountains.

We understand the means by which a change of heart in us is initiated. For the desire, the longing for spiritual enlightenment, even though it may sometimes be dominated by massive clouds of cruelty, oppression, distrust and fear, flows strongly below the surface.

First must come the realization of the survival of the human soul. From this knowledge is born a new wonder at the immensity and splendor of what we call God. Soon we're able to accept as normal the immanence of the heavenworld and conditions coincident to our own. Finally, we can look forward into the vistas of God's love for mankind, and know life in reality is love in expression.

All the different colors together make the spectrum of holiness, the sum total being the white light of the perfection of the Christ. In some measure this is given us to share. Through misinterpretation, we cut ourselves off from our brothers, living in seclusion, self-centeredness, self-concern. The light of Christ's holiness is a light of love. In it light streams from within, enveloping you in a garment of divine protection. The Christ is the beacon to guide men through darkness.

ESTHER BARNES During meditation I had a vision of a large, round-shaped entrance; it had all these diamonds, and it turned into a corridor. You'd walk down the corridor and see all these diamonds.

MARY That's the Court of the Doves in the Temple of Holiness. And you know the most beautiful thing is the ceremony when those white doves fly through. When the angels sing, it's beyond anything—I almost become emotional whenever I get into that picture and think on it, because it's quite the most wondrous thing, the angelic voices – and the rhythm of them stays with you.

MIRIAM WILLIS We speak of holy love, holy patience, holy stillness. And yet holiness isn't still, for it gives us strength to embrace everything that shines with the light of holiness. These thoughts can be in words, but many of them are filled with experiences which you've had, and your mind goes backward to them or forward in expectation, or dwells in a stillness in the vision of the present and of the holy presence.

When we climb the Channel, we could put the word "holy," if we wanted to, in front of every quality of the Channel, for we do stand, held in a holy faith in the glorious royal purple, and into all the other colors, onward and upward and over bridges until we reach the Fount of Supply, where we receive the infilling vitality and holiness of abundance in flowing color. Truly we stand on holy ground.

LORNA LANE At exactly 4 a.m. each morning – I look at the clock – I wake feeling and hearing this thud, and I have a sensation of landing, just plopping on my bed. I understand this is when I'm returning to my body from my night work.

MARY That's your reaction to the silver cord retracting into your body. Coming back, this happens because you haven't yet become accustomed to a soft landing. In time, the problem will take care of itself. You'll gradually learn how to come back more gracefully.

MIRIAM WILLIS This problem will go away in time, once we get to the point where we're more balanced; then that no longer happens.

GENE HAFFNER Question: how often do we see those we love on the other side? Is it just once in a while, or do we see them every night? Do we have to make a special effort to see them? Is anything required of them to see us?

MARY If that person is in a class with us over there, if that person desires to be developed and has a special tie with us, we see them every night that we go into a temple to study.

MIRIAM WILLIS Even if your loved ones are not in classes with us, Tuesday and Sunday nights, we're always free to see those to whom you have close ties. Just ask, and ye shall receive.

JOHN BRANCHFLOWER And do they see us, too?

MARY They certainly recognize us. Both they and we are in the spiritual body.

MARILYN I've been wanting confirmation of visiting with my family on the Other Side for a very long time. I take it on faith that we've met, that I'm seeing them at those special family gatherings Sunday and Tuesday nights, but I've never brought through a single recollection of it.

SYLVIA HOWE Isn't it true that they have to agree to see us, and some don't want to?

MIRIAM WILLIS Well, some have gone on to other areas of development and have no great ties left with us. They prefer to pursue their own paths and not revive the past, for better or worse. That said, most of our loved ones enjoy very much reuniting with us. Those who may not wish to are a minority, an exception.

SYLVIA Regarding what Marilyn said, some people have excellent recall of sharing time with their loved ones; others don't and wish they did, like Marilyn. It may take time for some people to be able to recall. But regardless, they're still developing in other, individual and important ways.

GLENN DIES And eventually, Marilyn may start recalling meeting her loved ones.

MARY As with everything we experience in these nighttime visits, at first we may not be conscious that anything is happening. For that reason, this training requires faith that endures until finally the seeker proves by his own experience.

DAN In our night sojourns, we encounter people from different groups on the Other Side. Mary isn't their teacher. So how do those people get there? Do they have another Earth teacher, or do they get to the Planes by other methods?

MIRIAM WILLIS Groups from all parts of the world take spiritual training on the Planes just as we do. Other Earth teachers besides Mary take students to the temples and halls of learning at night, and some individuals who visit the Planes may do so without an Earth teacher.

DAN But if they don't have an Earth teacher, then how do they get to the Planes?

MIRIAM WILLIS When the soul seeking higher consciousness is urged on by a desire to advance spiritually, that soul emits a radiant azure blue light which is seen by heavenly teachers in God's service. Such a teacher will respond to the call of the light shed by the soul, and invite him or her to go to the higher planes for growth and development. The soul will travel in the heavenly teacher's power and begin soul expansion and training on the Other Side. Thus, that soul can be picked up by a heavenly teacher and ride the steeps of heaven on the pathway of light, which will carry him to the temples of instruction.

DAN Will it be more difficult for that person remember his experiences seeing as he lacks an Earth teacher?

MIRIAM WILLIS Each individual responds according to his soul development. In our own case, we're fortunate to have Mary's help. And we have Color.

VIOLET Even if you don't bring back recollections, the teachings in these heavenly temples promote growth that you will eventually come to remember.

SYLVIA And the essence of what you experience is always impressing your soul, so that your Earth life will be affected in a profound way.

MARY If at first we may not be conscious that anything is happening, this training requires faith that endures until finally the seeker proves by his own experience.

EVE BRUCE I have a question about people who take psychedelics like LSD and magic mushrooms, and also people under anesthesia who die on the operating table and return to life – as in Near Death Experiences – to tell their recall of the tunnel experience: seeing the white light, seeing angels and other phenomena that many say changes them forever. So what I'd like to know: are these people experiencing the Planes of Heaven?

MIRIAM WILLIS They're going to a subplane. Some Near Death Experiences can be very strong emotional stimulants. Once the person returns to earth consciousness, they often find they're eager to seek greater spiritual development; then they may start going to the temples and halls of learning.

EVE What level would they be if they're starting out in this direction?

MIRIAM WILLIS The degree of soul development varies according to the person.

YVONNE (VONNIE) BRANCHFLOWER Where do people go when under sedation or having an operation under anesthesia?

MARY They go to what we would call a netherland. There's a great sleep land that is in the next registered realm or area, we'll say. And it's closer to the center, above the Magnetic Field on the 1st Plateau. They're "detained" as it were, "held." Sometimes they have vivid, pleasant dreams, sometimes ugly and unpleasant ones, depending on their reaction to however the dosage affects them.

MIRIAM ALBPLANALP If you take a sleeping pill what happens in your night work?

MARY It's a deterrent as far as the Planes are concerned. You're apt to be heavy in sleep. And an opiate keeps you here, earthbound.

PATTI I have a question about tie-ins, as relates to praying for another person.

MARY It's as if a line goes out and ties the person. It becomes a central radial power until the one for whom you're praying receives it. You can know when they receive it, because the light at your end goes out. You take a long breath and say, "It worked. Thank God it worked!"

MIRIAM WILLIS It's the soul call. And Color – color prayer would open the gate.

CAROL I'd like to ask a question about something I've heard you say, but I don't fully understand what you mean by "the three bodies."

MARY The physical, mental, and spiritual; we seek to develop perfect balance in our three bodies.

DORIS A question on auras. I was curious: did we improve our ability here? I thought I made some progress in that respect.

MARY The right to read an aura comes with the faith that God has given you the vision, and that in using that vision, you are uplifting the person whom you're reading.

MARGARET Some of us see partial auras, that is, we may see some color, especially around the head of another person. We know that being able to read a full aura belongs only to a highly developed person who's able to see and interpret the many, ever changing colors that extend for several feet around, above and even under the entire human being. I just wanted to mention this because I think there's some confusion and misinformation out there about auras, that some people believe an aura is static and is only halo of one shade. They don't realize how thoroughly dynamic and active an aura is.

MIRIAM WILLIS This is very true.

MIRIAM ALBPLANALP And not to forget that a master has seventeen permanent rays in his aura, a feat which we're trying to emulate in our own selves.

ESTHER BARNES I've been aware of the other world so many times in the last few months. It's just beyond my consciousness. I don't know how to describe it otherwise.

MARY Well, you're coming into the development of awareness, and remember, we wait to be awakened.

HELEN VON GEHR You know, I learn something every night. Just a picture of a stream and magnolia was so amazingly real and profound. It was a beautiful soul experience. I know I couldn't have accomplished the last few weeks if it hadn't been for the knowledge I gained here. It was just going with me everywhere I went. Color was right there, helping me every day.

MARY If with our morning tea or coffee, we could just say to ourselves, if this were my last day on Earth, what would I do? What one thing would I do to complete this one day? You'd be surprised. Some things that we have received as messages through the mirrors over there just before us, we do write that letter, or we apologize, or we make good something that we've left undone. In other words, we step right into that breach of promise as we have promised ourselves many times, before this day is over I'll write a word, I'll phone, I will try very hard to really make truth my standard.

VIOLET My vision and message: Flowing power, so strong that I felt as though lifted right up and off in space, as though I were being flown along with it. There was strength about me. It was purposeful and it had a destination, for I was traveling in a line on a definite course, not thrown about, but very steadily going forward. All this was being done to me; I had no say in the matter at all. So I just let myself go and felt buoyed and happy. This was an adventure that was being given me, and somehow I wanted it very much, so was content, relaxed, yet expectant. The air about me felt comfortable and was comforting.

Now I began to pass through an atmosphere more and more filled with luminous cloudlets, and there was a delicious perfume. It resembled nothing I could name, but it had life in it, and it was pleasant, perhaps like the ozone on the summit of very high mountains. My feet began to feel for a resting place. Very soon they touched ground, soft and smooth. I looked about me.

All I could see were those soft drifting clouds. In my mind, however, there was thought, as divine imagination began to take over. This gave me in wonderful vividness of perception a picture of the greatest Master, the Lord Christ. He was holding out his arms. Into them there seemed gathered all nations of the world being drawn to him as a shelter. The influence which flowed out from his presence was so marvelous that it had healing and uplift to still the multitude, until they became calm and could receive his blessing. And then each one moved away, to let a another man take his place near the Master, that he, too, might receive the blessing.

*****

REVIEW V
THE TRANSITION FROM
LIFE TO THE AFTERLIFE

The transition of "death" and life after life: what happens when we die? First, death is not an extinction; it is a welcoming into the fullness and richness of the Afterlife. Life and death are one coexistent reality. There is a hereafter where we live on in the many planes of Heaven. As Jesus said, "For in my Father's house are many mansions."

Dying is the death of all the darkening force of our nature. Living in the Afterlife is picking up the light. When we depart this world, crossing over to the other side to inhabit another dimension of reality, our consciousness goes along with us to the extent that we have developed it here on Earth. Lay up your treasure in Heaven. Our treasure goes over on waves of light. We only have what we send over.

When the silver cord is severed at death, the eternal part of us, the soul, leaves the body and very briefly passes over the Rim of Life. The discarnate is led through a primitive forest by heavenly guides. As he walks through this forest, stirred by the stillness and the beauty of it, ahead, he sees the River of Life. He steps down into the river and crosses it. Only seconds later, as he emerges from the water, he is washed clean and is perfectly dry.

He begins to climb toward the Landing Field of the 1st Plateau/ Subplane, the slowest vibrating dimension beyond the Earth plane. In a burst of light, he has arrived into glory, into the Kingdom of Heaven, an entrance filled with awe, amazing beauty and intensity. He is met by loved ones who are eagerly waiting to greet him. There are the invisible helpers, there are relatives, there are friends.

He is welcomed by his sponsor, a great soul who through many lives has taken the responsibility of guiding and helping a particular soul or a number of souls. It's a joyous occasion. He is received into the Kingdom; he is accepted; he knows no suffering, sin or wrong thinking. No person comes home to God who does not receive a welcome with outstretched arms. There will always be someone dear to you when you enter that Land. It is to this Plateau that the soul first goes, where we begin consciousness of our whereabouts, reckoning with who we are and what we can do with this life after life, now in the Afterlife.

This area caters to recovery, orientation and decisions. Centrally located above the Magnetic Field, the area helps souls become oriented to their new state of being. The first seven days in that world is an outpouring of love and understanding. And so, no matter how selfish a human is, how sinful or lost, they are human souls entering the Kingdom, and God has the respect for that soul, to give it entrance.

The Landing Field welcomes the new traveler amidst a joyful atmosphere and gets him started in the direction he will next go, to Restland. Here he stays in a happy atmosphere for seven days – and sometimes longer – which in effect is rest plus adjustment and preparation. No one is ever asked to leave Restland. You don't leave until you're ready. If the discarnate seems afraid to go on, if they've been in Restland too long, heavenly helpers try to move him along. Because a person can become quite fixed where they are.

The soul is enlivened for seven days, after which the earth consciousness to which it has been accustomed overtakes it. The consciousness that was so enlivened is forgotten, . It becomes so completely blotted out. If the discarnate has been sick, he reverts to that state of consciousness; if paralyzed, he is again paralyzed, unconscious or suffering, wanting old haunts and appetites, fighting or in shock, or whatever the predominating consciousness has been.

The soul reverts to this condition and goes to the Clearing Hospitals for healing. These Earth states of consciousness receive the most skilled and appropriate care and encouragement toward healing and cleansing in centers of consciousness administering to the ills of body, mind and soul.

When ready, the discarnate is taken to the Halls of Remembrance, where he will be able to read the plan of his just completed life on Earth. He is then taken to an area called Segregation, a place of revealing self to self, which poses testings and reflections from the life just lived; to Rhythmic Centers for further refinements, then to the Isle of Registration, where the life review will take place.

The Isle of Registration is divided into seven sections, including the Mirror of Life, where the self is truly reflected. There are seven mirrors in the Registration tests, clear mirrors and black mirrors. You stand before them and see what was positive and what was detrimental to you on Earth. No one tells you. You see it depicted there in those mirrors. We're shown our credits; you first see some very positive things about your life; then it's as if they're turned over to the other side and you see something quite different. You are unprepared for what you see; the reality is quite astonishing. We feel we should have known better in the first place. In other words, what you see next is contrary to what you originally saw. You see its opposite, the way you expressed a quality in a negative way.

There are just as many things you did well, but when you step away from that mirror, there's no memory of what you've done that was right; it's what you haven't done right that you remember. Possibly the life of someone else could be affected by something that we deliberately did. At the time it didn't impress us, but now we have to forgive ourselves and forgive others.

Registration and the Mirror of Life remind us of our shortcomings, unheeded truths and the lack of fulfillment in our lives. You register your fears, your hatreds, your loves --- everything is registered there. Registration involves passing seven tests before one can advance. Placing one's own limits on oneself, we are judged by ourselves.

One is handed two blueprints: what your life could have been and what your life actually was, and you begin to look at your Earth life under closer scrutiny. And this is where reincarnation may come in for those who are ready to look that far back. You can see that right through all your lives the same thing turned up over and over again.

On then to the Examining Field, fourteen tests, and further rhythmic centers to give to us needed strength and stability. When the newly arrived soul is ready, he will gravitate to the heavenly plane he has earned. The plane we earn from development in our Earth life will become our home in the Afterlife.

*****

> ## FOURTH STEEP To the AREA and TEMPLE OF SELFLESSNESS, TEMPLE OF BALANCE
>
> First Station: RECOMPENSE One is empowered to see and correct imbalances in relationships before going higher. This includes Retribution where we're penitent. We correct our errors and imbalance. We're conscious of the difficult Path. Restitution:. we make amends to another, apologize or repay in goods or service. Restoration. We restore condition or relationship, through love.
>
> Second Station: POWER The principal ego becomes the instrument through which the law of the universe can become enacted. This power subdues the carnal ego, frees the spiritual ego, balances the earth child with the heavenly child within.
>
> Third Station: LOVE here is a reaffirmation of the power and wisdom within creative love force; tests of selfless love given, any remaining bigotry cleared.
>
> Fourth Station: WISDOM is the aspect of the God-self which knows what is good or true and what is not. It makes love wise, and raises thought above the merely mental realm. Here we develop the stability of the faculty needed.
>
> Fifth Station: BALANCE considers in all directions without losing polarity.
>
> Sixth Station: PEACE is the stillness at the center of one's being in love made manifest. In human affairs. Peace ranges from Earth-level absence of overt war to the spiritual peace that passeth understanding.

******

AREA AND TEMPLE OF SELFLESSNESS

MIRIAM WILLIS When we reach the brink of the 9th Plane, we've climbed to a height of consciousness, and sometimes, to our great sorrow, we're not conscious of the experience of the soul, the touch of the divine spirit, as fully as we'd wish to be. How well we know this great feeling of longing, to be lured on into the higher consciousness of these great gifts and opportunities that the Father has bestowed upon us in our night sojourns.

So let's ask to quicken the inner ears of our being, the inner eyes of our soul, that all dimness may be washed away in the living waters of vitality, and ascend to a sensitivity in our desire to be aware of the slightest glimmer of light and illumination that filters into our consciousness, and in the recognition of it, to give it voice within our being, something we can hold dear and share. And in the sharing we can rejoice. In the discipline of the holding force of our patience, love, clothed in the royal purple of faith, we continue on.

Let us follow the lighted pathway up that mountain. Always it seems to be a zigzag. It must be so; otherwise it would be too steep and we'd slip backward. These are similar to the Steeps of Heaven we encountered on the Eightfold Path, where we were encouraged to become more like unto the Master, having the qualities of his divine nature transform the qualities within us that need refining. So as we climb the zigzag path, let us express gratitude every step of the way for having been brought thus far, for having been helped to overcome when we've slipped back; for having been given a glimpse of the divine light, and let us give thanks for the many blessings we have.

As we're near the top, let us feel in our imagination, and then in reality, that exhilaration of lightness that comes in suspended consciousness. We feel the warmth and radiance of the infilling of light, the lift of power, the joy of conscious love and of divine communion. Gratitude takes away any heaviness that would drive us down.

And here we are at the top of the mountain. We see great vistas. We thank God for the temples we go to each night of the week, for the reflected beauty, the wisdom and love that filters in through our day in a thousand different of ways.

To the height of this mount in the glow of divine love, let us open the receptivity of our inner being, and even at this height climb higher, infilling every ray of the Channel of our inner being with infinite love and power. At the Fount of Supply, the very floodgates of the generosity of divine love flowing over us is a baptism of spirit.

Our preparation brings us to the Area and Temple of Selflessness with a buoyancy of faith that causes us to feel joy and confidence. We've walked out of cramped quarters into a vast area of freshness and rebirth. On this upsurge of seeking, we begin the various tests of self, revealing motives and actions.

We continue such testing for thirty days, not only seeing the truth concerning ourselves in our night sojourns, but also carrying through this knowledge in day to day living of our earth lives.

We discover that the greatest tests of selflessness manifest in living with our fellow man, and the measuring rod, the standard of selflessness, is patterned in the life of the Master. Thus the Area of Selflessness must become our area of attainment. In these tests we're shown again how the use of Color can ease the way and advance our growth.

MARY Faith in one's self is such an important lesson. The keystone of the arch that marks the universal way is individual responsibility within the plan of unchanging law. Throughout nature, the basic law is that for every action, there is an equal and opposite reaction. That's the Law of Compensation, the impersonal guiding force of matter and spirit, the karmic principle of self-knowledge. Its administrator is the soul itself, inseparable from the all embracing, divine soul of the universal God-consciousness. Its role in human destiny is measured by the seeker's conscious awakening to an objective realization of his place in the divine plan.

VIOLET We'd be talking now about the 10th Ray of the Spiritual Arc of Green, that lovely. soft sea foam green, meaning "awareness of sowing and reaping, expanding in conscious understanding."

MARGARET It signifies the relentless rhythm of the great ocean tides, for this ray embodies the Law of Compensation: "whatsoever a man sows, so shall he reap," what comes in must go out, where there's cause there's effect.

ESTHER BARNES This ray helps the seeker to be receptive to the inflowing currents of soul wisdom to replace ego-centered concepts.

MIRIAM ALBPLANALP Those who use this ray are expanding their higher consciousness and transforming their thinking. The 10th Ray of the Spiritual Arc of Green is a balancing ray that encourages growth that challenges one to new goals and helps one recognize unrewarding patterns.

MARY Through the depth of seeing into the heart of man, having a greater endowment of insight to read ourselves and our brother fairly and truly, we realize we have the consciousness to come back from that world to this world, bringing with us something that seems to envelop us, an understanding. And so we're the larger and the more informed as we take one test after the other.

MIRIAM WILLIS And as you know, when our souls are given tests in the higher realms, we'll have a parallel test in our physical life. These tests are a means of unfolding consciousness. The higher the plane, the more difficult the test.

MARY Through the training in the Area and Temple of Selflessness, the seeker demonstrates that he was given a power to pursue love and its handmaidens – wisdom, balance, and peace – in order to manifest into the true light and bring forth the spiritual light of God's illuminating energy from which spiritual consciousness grows. No man can escape his responsibility to himself to release that which is within his plan of life, namely, an unfolding expression of the blueprint he came into this life with. He must realize his potential in order to objectively fulfill what his soul intuitively knows.

Believe and accept the spiritual, cosmic world. Behold, its towers reach unto a new consciousness of sight and hearing unlimited by time or space. Light from the Father; love from the son; power from the holy spirit, all three are the manifestation of God. Light can only change the darkness when we let it in. Love can only change our dungeon when we clear it out. Light is the conqueror of darkness in the soul, the body, the spirit; this is the spiritual chemical scientists say lies beyond and behind all findings and analyses. Light – God – they are the same.

MIRIAM WILLIS This planet begins to feel the dim consciousness of man awakening in a new aspect of awareness beyond the three dimensions of sense perception. There is one universal love, light, going forth again in ever active cycles of intelligent revelation. The different colors together make the spectrum of holiness, the sum total being the white light of the perfection of the Christ, of love, of selfless giving and power.

The light of Christ's holiness is a light of love. In it light streams from within, enveloping you in a garment of divine protection. The Christ is the beacon to guide men through the darkness. Purify your soul; fill it with light. Open the door of your heart. It takes courage and love with trust that steps out fearlessly, braving the storm to bask in the sunshine of interior peace. And from light we receive inspiration.

ROSEMARY I had an unfortunate falling out with a friend, an estrangement which has now lasted some two, nearly three years. From time to time I think about it, trying to better understand. This week, I had an experience in the Temple of Selflessness, in which I saw this friend from whom I'm estranged. I caught fleeting glimpses of her on different floors in a tall building. Each time, I succeeded in avoiding contact by quickly escaping to another floor just in the nick of time. I didn't want to risk unpleasantness with her. But finally, it was no longer possible to evade her; and we had no choice but to acknowledge one another.

Upon waking the next morning, I not only recalled but literally relived the experience of this heaven world contact, in which my friend was crying very deep, heart rending sobs. I could feel her warm tears on my own cheeks. Our heads were right next to one another, touching; it was as if I were comforting her weeping, and as if our thoughts were melding. She was murmuring, "I'm so sorry, I shouldn't have said the things I did. I don't know why I get so angry and mean, why I take it out on other people, like you."

I've searched my soul these past years of separation from her, wondering what I could have done to avoid the split between us. I've been afraid to contact her, because when provoked, she has a bad temper, she can be sarcastic and biting, she twists others' words – and I just haven't wanted to get into another no-win situation with her. But now, because of the temple experience, I do understand her much better and I feel a compassion toward her that I didn't have before.

I feel this temple experience was telling me that deep down, my friend is sorry for what happened between us. What I experienced in the temple was like an apology from her. But having been raised Catholic, well taught by the nuns, I learned the Act of Contrition, in which we promise God to "avoid all sin and near occasions of sin."

My friend and I were in tune on the Other Side, but on the physical plane, I'm still wary of being exposed to her again. I think of my Catholic Act of Contrition, of avoiding "all near occasions of sin," so as to not open myself up to a chance of further negativity by contacting her, which could be a "near occasion of sin." At the same time, this temple experience was a very beautiful beginning of my understanding, seeing the vulnerability of her innermost being exposed that way. I was very grateful for this experience. It was deep and meaningful and told me so much. I realize I still have a lot to resolve, but this temple experience made a huge impression.

MARY Sometimes we're given experiences of misunderstanding just so that we're to have our eyes opened, that we may grow in stature when it comes to correcting things, when they're in the lives of people whom we see are walking too close to the edge of the abyss of misunderstanding. One can go over that edge so quickly! And the suffering that goes with it is poignant. So I have a feeling that if you believe you haven't wronged anyone, then God and you have an understanding. And if you feel that you have, you have to realize that there are many people that wouldn't stand for your apologizing. Pride is the wall between you at that time. I believe that someday that wall will be broken down. If our hearts are pure and we still keep praying for people who have misunderstood, again, look closely at yourself and ask, was I dominating the situation? Did I in any way move too far?

I know that if you can look back in your lives and see that there was no anger, no jealousy, no distrust, you can wipe everything off the slate. Then say, "This has happened to me to make me more of an understanding person, and I'll watch to see where I can help someone else."

MIRIAM Pray on it, dear. You'll certainly find the answers you're seeking.

MARY On these Planes we have so many great Prayer Stations where our prayers, taken in color, can be activated. We find that prayer is not for naught; it has its answer; your prayer is answered many times while you're saying it. Don't be afraid to pray if you have something that's bothering you. We all can afford that prayer. And if we could once realize how in doing that, we're building a structure of protection around us.

KATHY We've spoken of prayer in the context of what it's wise to pray for. I know better than to pray for a new Cadillac or to win the lottery. Instead, what I've prayed for, and still do, is order. I had this only too frequent feeling of my life being in disorder. So I prayed for order, and I received several experiences on the Other Side that helped me to effect desired changes in my life. Many of these experiences were symbolic, where upon waking, I recognized the symbols immediately as being cues to my subconscious. When the changes I was praying for began to manifest, I knew it was the answer to prayer – effected by my work on the Other Side. I recognized the miracle of divine help.

BARBARA STONE As we face ourselves in the 9th Plane Area of Selflessness, we're consciously searching for any threads of selfishness. We find strange elements we haven't hitherto realized. We discover that oversensitivity is really selfishness. Overemphasis on anything relating to the self is basically selfish: the way people affect us; the over-awareness of others' opinions of us; a stressing of our own personal opinions – all these are phases of the same prominence of the self, because such a state is one of separation. This is one of the lessons learned here.

MIRIAM WILLIS One's life is examined very carefully, and one is checked up on any of these areas where the motive has been for selfish self gain. Necessary corrections are realized under the searchlight of self analysis. Here is where selfless desire is learned, and we bathed in that lovely, soft lettuce green.

VIOLET This Area has many sections with little courts or meditation patios. In each there is beauty of a pool and some architectural feature symbolizing the subjective process to be realized. There's a planting of shrubs and flowers, fountains, water spots, a contrast of light and shade. There's an assembly area in the center where talks are given to make clear the transformation of physical endowments into the spiritual. The realization aligns to a soul that's deeply in earnest.

MARY Let us rise above the "normal" to the strata of Color, above the level of lower thinking. Get rid of hatreds here. Hatreds and biases are bad habits. If you're going through an experience now, you can be sure it's in your path. Take in the overcoming; we're rewarded. If a door is closed to us, that door opens a double door. Close the door of anger, dislike, impatience, criticism.

Criticism is one of the most expensive traits. It's the feeling that our ego is superior. Criticism often comes from certain nervous worries. Release yourself from criticism, let yourself come clean and start anew. Impatience is the handmaiden of criticism. Perfectionists are impatient people, aren't they? Impatience is a most trying thing that we have to contend with. What we want is the thing to happen right now. Temper and anger make blocks in the nervous system to overcome. The other person has rights. When you go down to the level of anger you're as low as anyone. Be patient with people, patient with yourself.

All right, you've made progress in your meditations, your calculations in life and your spiritual uplift. Just one overflowing moment when nothing is right, and you're telling all the world about it is shrieking out, breaking down all the tender filaments you created through the chemical change of your thinking. We mix most of our thought with troublesome thoughts. Violent thoughts, emotional thoughts. We forget to be thankful.

The uselessness of letting our dispositions, through emotionalism, just get all out of joint – strike out here and strike out there. We make a small turn and find ourselves in a dilemma, a sort of detour. Then all of a sudden, we seem to have clearer sight and feel the call within.

We go to different parts of the temples, and after the group sessions end, we're on our own. We really were called to come to that place. We make entrance into a grotto, we go in and wait our turn. Sometimes the lesson we learn is simple, but much needed. And these lessons so many times come up later in our life as we study and go along in this work. We're presented with something that goes way back. It may even seem like nothing. So it does pay us to keep track of what we dream or what comes suddenly to us; whether we're meditating or when we're lost in thought, something comes out that's brilliant, and that's our answer. It's a state of reality that we bring away with us.

It's these little fallacies seem to follow us that trip us up. When we lose control, the spiritual aura disappears. Who has the right to be intolerant? One-of the simple fallacies of development is thinking you're tolerant. Very few people are." Tolerance helps us to attain lasting changes in soul development.

GEORGE FLOURNOY Is there a color for tolerance? Or could you give us a plume?

MIRIAM WILLIS Mary did give us a plume for tolerance. Start with dark green, then on to slightly greenish yellow, to delft blue; add a center stripe or bridge of dead old rose to make the quality die; then wild rose and lavender smoke.

MARGARET We also have the 12th Ray of the Spiritual Arc of Red: soft-greyed old rose, meaning "a universal concept of life, tolerant, understanding, seeing God in all creation, recognizing the One Source in manifold forms."

MIRIAM WILLIS The power of this ray is reinforced as a particular aid in our Earth lives.

MARY Tolerance comes with developing this 12th ray in the aura. Like others of the red spiritual rays, this one helps us to attain lasting changes in soul development. There enters into the life a rich appreciation of inner and outer realities, a transcending that reaches out in wordless praise. One grows in ability to sense, then to realize many degrees of vibration. With this maturing sensitivity, one feels and knows that God is everywhere, within all that is, comforting and blessing us with this delicate color.

VIOLET I received this in the Temple of Selflessness: "The purpose of life is to find the perfect expression of our true selves. In our search to discover the purpose of life, observing the imperfections of our currently inadequate expressions, we learn that the purpose of life is to discover the meaning of life; and while each life, through its individual expression, has its own meaning, all meanings lead finally to the infinite source, the divine consciousness we call God."

ANDREW HOWE We have a tall order before us for one lifetime.

BILL ESTABROOK A good reason we reincarnate. But how many lives does it take? How many incarnations do we need till we reach "the ultimate"?

MARGARET It's my understanding that if you achieve being a 20th Plane soul here on Earth, you have a choice of deciding whether to incarnate again to live another life here, or choosing to continue your development on the Other Side.

MIRIAM WILLIS In each experience given you in these temples on the Planes, you as an evolving soul develop faculties and capacities, leaving less to be attained when you enter life eternal.

WILLARD STONE Why do they call it "life eternal" if we're going to reincarnate? Isn't that a contradictory, misleading term?

BERNARD BURRY It's neither contradictory nor misleading, because from one life to the next, as we reincarnate, our consciousness never dies, our consciousness is eternal. We are eternal souls.

The myth of the "death of consciousness" has been perpetuated because people identify with the physical body, falsely assuming that since the body perishes, conscious intelligence disappears as well. However, consciousness exists outside the constraints of time and space. Intelligence existed prior to matter. Consciousness created the material universe, not vice versa.

At death, energy is released from the body and our consciousness goes with it. Consciousness, which is nonmaterial, continues after the death of the physical body.

FRANK Think also of the Law of Conservation of Energy and Matter, which states that energy and matter can be neither created nor destroyed, but can only be changed in form. That tells you life is eternal.

JOHN BASINSKI: Quantum theory is another indicator. Life doesn't end when the body dies, at "death;" our consciousness moves to another dimension. Consciousness and intelligence, existed prior to matter. A form of consciousness or intelligence creates the material universe, not the other way around.

FRANK The so-called death exists as a concept because people identify themselves with their physical body, and wrongfully believe because the body perishes, their consciousness will disappear, too.

But consciousness doesn't end with the death of the physical body. Consciousness, the non-material part of you, lives on after the death of the physical body.

VIOLET It's a wonderful thing when this becomes a part of the knowing soul, a part of the deepest you.

MARY That other world is all around us, it interpenetrates at different points. You can stand with a loved one who comes, and their aura interpenetrates yours, both here and there.

MIRIAM WILLIS It's a state of spiritual consciousness.

MARY One world without end, amen.

ESTHER ESTABROOK Haven't we been told that it's far easier to develop on Earth than to do so over there?

FRED ADLER Yes. Because on Earth we face challenges that develop us more easily and quicker, because heaven is a peaceful place, no friction like we have here on Earth. And like it or not, we learn many lessons from friction and conflict.

MICHAEL We learn from suffering. As we know from the Eightfold Path.

WILLARD STONE Mary has told us that five years of development on Earth is equal to twenty years development on the Other Side. So those of us who live long lives are blessed to be given the time to devote to spiritual growth.

CARMEN AUSTIN (CHRISTINE ADLER) But of course, there's no finality! There is ongoing continuity of life and death. We have all lived before and we will live again. We all know that.

ANDREW HOWE I find it interesting that belief in reincarnation goes back as far as there are records, that the ancient Hebrews originally accepted but later repudiated it because of the hated Roman conquerors' espousal of it. Christianity embraced reincarnation until some of the early church fathers, for political reasons, decided to anathematize it. But despite the efforts of the powers that be, people never stopped believing in reincarnation. The conviction of its truth seems to be a profound reality in our innermost fabric, and today, the majority of people on the planet accept it.

WILLARD More than 90% of Earth's population believes in reincarnation. It must be something within us, an innate knowing.

EVELYN SWANSON Could you explain what "staying over there permanently" means, and how the concept of "permanently" relates to reincarnation?

MARY It means that after you pass over, you'll stay on the Other Side for quite a long time before the rounds come up again, when you'll be eligible to reincarnate if you wish. Not everyone wishes, not everyone needs to live another life. You may have accomplished everything you needed to accomplish that Earth can teach. Conversely, though you may not need another lifetime, you may want to return for a special cause or mission. We use the term "permanent" because the interval over there, after having lived here, is a fairly long time. But it may not be permanent in the sense of "forever."

EVELYN You say "quite a long time." How long would that be, exactly?

MARY The usual interval until the rounds come up again is about one hundred years. The length of time between, the teachers tell me, is anywhere from a hundred years on up.

ESTHER BARNES I received a teaching on this subject that I wrote down. If I may read it to the class: "One who is ready to reincarnate is taken to the Temple of Reincarnation to prepare him for his sojourn on Earth. Here he learns what the plan of his life will be when the soul takes up his new life. The final decision is made for the time of rebirth into the Earth; preparations ensue, and many visits are made to this Temple of Reincarnation prior to the actual rebirth itself. With permission, we may go here to read from what was given in the Akashic records, in order to talk over with our heavenly teachers gleanings from our past lives and decisions for our future ones."

AVIS   Could you say something about Akasha and the Akashic Records, Mary?

MARY   Akasha has been described as the all-pervasive life principle of the universe, a universal medium in which everything is contained. It fills all space and interpenetrates all matter. Indian philosophy interprets Akasha as ether, the subtlest element that permeates the universe. Buddhists and Hindus say Akasha is space that is bounded by the material world, an infinite, indefinable space that contains the material world. Historical records of all events and experiences, of all thoughts and actions that have ever taken place, are taking place and will take place are indelibly imprinted upon Akasha. The Akashic records are read by adepts and initiates. Akashic records are on the 2nd, 4th and 5th Planes. We view the Akashic Records, in our night work in different temples, seeing what we've accumulated in past lives and what we have for our record this life.

Someone said to me this week, "Why do you spend so much time thinking about the other life? All I can do is take care of the life here." I believe we're thinking about the "other" life in order to find the plan of our own life in the here and now, and to go along in harmonious living; then we're more able to enjoy life here, and not eternally see the fault in the other person. That's selflessness, to a degree.

People who are changing their lives to a more perfect pattern start within. It's the withinness of ourselves where we begin cleaning house, perfecting what's ours. And I'll say to you again: written upon your soul when you came into this world was the plan of your life. A great architect etched on that soul that plan. Each of us has a unique Plan of Life that our higher self has selected for our individual spiritual development and ongoing, toward which we're given infinite chances through living succeeding lives to perfect. It's a sign of wisdom to give thought to the next life and to seek mastery in both worlds.

As you've climbed through these Planes up to the 9th, you've had experiences on the Eightfold Path that were hard to take. I believe that was in your Plan of Life. This is the way we reach out and find the remedy for the mistakes we've made.

GERTRUDE CLARK   Is there a secret of how to find our life plan?

MARY   You're given that Plan not from any teacher, but through your own effort, your own prayer and meditation and your faith and belief that life is right, because God's in his heaven.

I believe we're given the strength to go through almost anything that's given us to go through. I believe that in living this everyday life, we're sowing the seeds and replenishing the work, that it may move on into the hearts of others. Let's keep this before us, if there's just one ray of harmony through every day, we're building stepping stones to reality.

LOLA   In letting emotions get the upper hand, what about the emotion of over concern or the feeling of great sympathy for another who's suffering? Is that type of emotion one that will break down the progress of a person?

MARY   No, it isn't in self pity, it isn't in doubt or fear. It's for someone else, for a brother. That's brotherly love. I don't think we can ever criticize it. Love is and always will be. We were born into this world to know love and to practice it; to evolve to being loving. The pathos of people who do not know love, to be without that desire for happiness for other people, to selfishly go on... a man can have everything, but if he doesn't know love, he's barren. You say to me, "There are many kinds of love." All right! Then let him know one of those loves. Let him give of himself in some way.

A few words says, "And God took the wanderer by the hand and led him to the water, and he drank strongly, and he became healed." Now if we could believe that, that by drinking of the waters of life that there is healing, instead of troublesome things happening eternally to us. We forget to be thankful, don't we? Let us ask ourselves: was there one proof of God's love in your life this week? Outstanding proof that you could reckon with? Write it down.

ESTHER BARNES Right here, right now, we're experiencing proof of God's love in our lives, just by being here, listening, learning, being a part of the power that's blessing us all.

MARY The Channel is between you and the knowledge of that other world that is your eternal home. Whether you want to or not, your time will come. And in the rounds of life you will realize happiness both here and over there. To go into that reality, that other world as an enlightened person is something so great that I expect all of you to realize everything that you have done in these classes.

And I know that if you were deprived of the right to think on these things you would immediately begin to search to know, write out all you know, or to give all you know to someone else. Because to be deprived is something that no man can stand easily. And the deprivation of many people who realize these things and have no outlet and no chance to speak without offense, and the offense is one of fear on the part of the person that can't receive it.

Because, after all, it's a big responsibility which changes the thinking of any person – or to make them discontented with what they have. And I don't believe I have any right to take one thought or one building block away from a person unless I can replenish or refurnish the block to go back in, of a lighter, brighter material. If I can do that, then I'm building. Life building was the plan of our great Creator. That great architect of the universe showed us that he had this knowledge of the great building of this kingdom of his on earth. Step by step, we're becoming more ready to receive what he gives us. (At least some of us are). Let us be one of the enlightened ones.

VIOLET Mary, I'd like to say that what you've been saying has been very interesting to me, because it's given the answer to some of the things that happened in my life – why they happened.

HELEN von GEHR. It seems to me that here – this room, this house, this class – is a center of peace. We come here and a peace settles upon us, we get our visions, our inspiration, and we have a fellowship, a love that is unique and beautiful, and we're very grateful for it.

ROWENA MEEKS We spoke of building blocks, and that reminded me of the picture I saw of a pyramid. I was wondering about it when an angelic being took me by the hand and opened a door, and I went in. I looked around and the being wasn't there any more, but I was told I must seek myself.

MARY Sooner or later, everyone becomes a seeker. All of us here are on the quest. And as you go out on this platform of faith, you'll find there are stairways leading to this person and that. And coming up the stairs they will greet you and ask questions.

ETHEL In this temple I received the message that what the world needs today is love, faith in each other, and to have a cause to believe in and make it thrive and grow.

RALPH I saw figure eights, several of them. And a cross.

MARY Figure eight is two worlds, is it not? You are at the union of two worlds. There must be a decision, a worldly decision, first, to start with. And it you were relieved of some of the worldly decisions you would have made time for. Is that not true?

RALPH Yes.

MARY Your figure eights would be that to me. The cross is the thing that we ever carry with us. Every man bears his cross. Every man is a cross. And with the head lifted we become Christ on the cross. So every man bears his cross. And as he becomes enlightened his head is held higher. And he is a seeker. To become a seeker is something that imbues man with a God like substance. He has so much to give. He's never hungry, because he receives. And as ye give ye shall receive.

BARBARA I came back one morning with the remembrance that a woman handed me a gold parchment that seemed to shine. On it was a message about my husband. She said, "We've been praying for him, and everything is going to be all right." I remember reading the whole thing, and the words stood out very clearly. She wanted me to notice the name that was on there. It was her name, "Methal." And then there was a more personal message regarding my husband on the bottom of that little sheet.

MARY Let us give God the glory for all that we receive each day of our lives. I was told – I don't often repeat what I was told – but I was told that great conflict in the Far East, the shadows were deepening, things were getting very hard there – that was about two weeks ago. And it struck a sort of a fear through me. And then in one of the temples, someone asked the question, "Do you believe that we people of the Earth will ever see peace?"

And a great angelic chorus took up the word "peace." So let us hold that in our hearts. God, let the aura of peace be around us. May we behold the vision of those we can help. May the scales of darkness be taken from our eyes, that the auric life may be shown to us. Amen.

The Area of Selflessness brings a great significance to the soul of the need to plumb its depths to discover hidden treasures that have contributed to present development, and in this stabilized strength, to cast light an the dark areas of selfishness. Through Color and through the faith, you're having revealed to you what is that next world. And so, if our little group does nothing but share the power of belief that we do not die, we just go on living, the continuance of life is on the Other Side, that we move along in development and beauty... we have shared a great truth.

*****

TEMPLE OF BALANCE

In the Temple of Balance, one sees the causes of his imbalance and is given power to grow to truer balance. He is taught how to recreate his forces, to become more poised and controlled in his emotions so that he learns to live in balance of body, mind and soul.

MIRIAM WILLIS Fear is a source of imbalance. But in this Temple of Balance, we're trained in being centered to keep on the power ray in leaving the body at night and living in balance by day, freed from moods of depression, criticism, bias and prejudice. Here one grows in the desire to live in radiance.

MARY "Build within you an altar of Faith." Enter the great silence in quietness and confidence. Balancing our forces causes us to become selfless. When man's spiritual perception is unfolded and he attains self knowledge, he will live in balance and thus attain the consciousness of his own immortality. Jesus Christ has bridged the chasm between man and God. Following him, we can't lose our way. Spiritual illumination comes to man where he lives in harmony, earning the right to walk the path of light.

Through countless ages man has wandered, yearning to find the soul's direction. At last there stretches before him the broad, wide path of knowledge, and he need wander no more. He follows the footsteps of the Master, serenely aware of the divine plan of his life. As the result of living in balanced faith, great visions of spirit are given him; visions overshadow him with the rainbow of the reality of God's love. He knows that only by balancing his "three bodies" can he hope for happiness. He also comes to realize, "from the crushed grapes of sorrow, the wine of inspiration is extracted."

As it follows the path of action, the awakened soul is ever seeking to express beauty in mind and body. This is what faith and gratitude will do. It simply works magic: you bloom, bringing healing to body and mind. Spiritual pioneers from the dark ages to the present have fought their way through dense forests of ignorance, prejudice and fear, ever keeping their eyes toward the vision of man's liberation from the prison of his own making. Love and truth, handmaidens of faith, walk hand in hand.

The Temple of Balance gives us the law, and brings us back to basic principles and harmony, teaching man to realize life in terms of forces rather than form.

The color of "Longing," one part of the 1st Ray of the Spiritual Arc of Purple, is a soft grey lavender. It's the entrée to the world of spiritual balance, and it leads to achieving the next step higher.

The law of balance is unalterable cosmic law, the spiritual law of the soul. The polarization or harmonious union of the opposite poles of life forces is the law of creation from the atom to man and superman, and life in all its expressions is a great marriage song. The whole message is given in music, the vibratory humming of the life forces in which every atom of our being is singing its own song. We're like great orchestras whose keynote sounds in the middle of our body. According to our realization of this truth does the orchestra give forth tones of beauty that transmute discord into harmonious music. As man becomes a seeker and goes forth in quest of truth, the birth of the new man takes place. Man has taken the silent path of wisdom; his heart has communed through love; he attains rebirth of the soul.

VIOLET Nothing is forced upon anyone. God doesn't punish us, nor does he take us by the hand and lead us; but he showed us through the Christ how we might find happiness. And today the chaos in the world can be very quickly relieved if every man could find his portion of harmony within himself. This is what Christ came to show us – that man can reach illumination through union of mind and spirit. When we're in the Channel and during meditation, we achieve conscious union and at-one-ment with God, our creator.

JEANNE I had a water test in the Temple of Balance that occurred in a large body of water seeming without beginning or end. A heavenly teacher was guiding me to brave these waters, which were very rough with a scary undertow that really scared me. My task was to retrieve a large silver cup in the middle of these troubled waters. I doubted I would be able to accomplish it. The water was so dark and dangerous, the waves were so high, and I was stark in the middle of it. I could see no horizon or shore, I was just stranded, stuck in a vast ocean, struggling to stay alive, not knowing how I was going to get out of this awful predicament. I really felt like I was going to die.

Lovingly and with great patience, the teacher encouraged me so that eventually, to my surprise, I succeeded in embracing the cup. It was actually easy once I gave up the struggle and listened to guidance. The waters calmed, they became peaceful, and I could now not only see the horizon and the shore, but believe I could swim to land. It was almost a miraculous transformation, and the process was very spiritual.

ESTHER BARNES That test seems so absolutely clear ... she was tested on fear and overcame it.

ESTHER ESTABROOK What a wonderful experience. It shows how that world over there really cares about us and wants to help us.

MARY It's by alignment to the unshakeable, indestructible conviction of universal, eternal spiritual life that man is born of spirit and therefore is spirit. Open to the eternal worlds, open the immortal eyes inwards into the worlds of eternity, ever expanding the human imagination in the bosom of God. Spirit divine, pour upon man thy vision of the seeker.

*****

REVIEW VI
THE PSYCHOLOGICAL AND SPIRITUAL RAYS OF MARY'S CREATIVE COLOR ANALYSIS

The basic foundation for Mary Weddell's Planes of Heaven classes was Mary's unique and elegant "Creative Color Analysis" course. The Color teaching was an integral component of our Planes experience, complementing it beautifully.

We live in a universe powerfully designed by color, whose energy is both visible and invisible. The Color Path is a mystical journey toward development of the soul. It is the way of illumination and intuitive perception. In Mary's classes and in those taught by Mary's senior teacher Miriam Willis, students explored color with emphasis on the etheric rays of the invisible world, which become visible when our higher senses are attuned.

In the invisible world are many octaves of light. Just as each color has its own individual wave length, so each has a message and a special effect. Mary's color teaching totals more than 100 basic rays, and is composed of psychological colors, spiritual colors, and extended rays, each with its separate meaning and power. The fully tested etheric color rays Mary brought through from the Other Side consist of the following five basic Spiritual Arcs of Color with 12 rays each:

The Spiritual Arc of Green – "Growth"
The Spiritual Arc of Red – "Metamorphosis"
The Spiritual Arc of Blue – "Training of the Ego"
The Spiritual Arc of Yellow – "Illumination"
The Spiritual Arc of Purple – "Spiritual Balance"

Four Psychological Arcs, Green, Red, Blue and Yellow, 12 rays each; Plus a number of "Extended Rays."

Many of these colors are not simply shades, hues or tints, but combinations of colors containing midrays, or colors described as either "streaked with", "tipped with," "touched with," "dirtied with," "overlaid with," "underlaid with," "with side shadings," "striated," "striped," or "swirling." Since Mary saw the colors in forms of a feather, she called the color combinations "fans," "arcs," and "plumes."

Mary saw her Color teaching as stepping stones to self realization, knowledge, spiritual development, cosmic attunement, and understanding of how to apply universal law in everyday life, so that we might realize our rightful inheritance to live compassionate lives in wisdom, health, harmony, abundance, peace and love. She believed that the knowledge of long-lost color meanings revealed to her and her development in the skill of using color were harmonious with what Jesus taught his disciples, when he took them apart and taught them many things. "Color is the path taught by Christ and by other great teachers," Mary said. "In the study of Color, our admonition is love."

So Mary's Color course involves soul searching, seeking, finding and traveling along that lighted pathway that protects us so greatly and expands our whole life and brings us finally to spiritual maturity.

*****

> ### FIFTH STEEP - To THE TEMPLE OF THE SEEKER, TEMPLE OF ILLUMINATION
>
> First Station: DISCIPLINE This requires yielding the will and the emotions to the soul's desire to fulfill its high destiny.
>
> Second Station: ALERTNESS. Alertness is keen awareness. One must be alert to higher guidance, to the needs of others, to the needs of one's own situation. To the NOW.
>
> Third Station: PATIENCE is a mesa of Consciousness, creating within the seeker a poised stillness.
>
> Fourth Station: RELAXATION releases the flowing rhythm of Spirit in which one functions naturally in this higher octave of expressed development.
>
> Fifth Station: SERENITY is peace of soul that sheds clear light on the lens of human reflection.
>
> Sixth Station: STABILITY is the result of establishing the higher octave of consciousness in the life.

****

TEMPLE OF THE SEEKER

In this temple of vast proportions, we're aware of great heights. We read over the gates at the entrance of the temple: "Man's great work is himself. His place of operation is wherever he finds himself, and his tools are the means at hand."

MIRIAM WILLIS I was looking over the charts to discover the temples and areas that are particularly marked by seeking, and it seemed to me the whole climb of the Planes is one of seeking. Our night work – isn't that a seeking? Isn't it a great seeking on the part of humanity for the power of God to bless, for us to discover all the wonderful creative things that are displayed in the heaven world that we can see.

We begin to feel a transforming quality in the phrase, "My yoke is easy, my burden is light." In the comparison of two aspects – the light of knowing and the darkness of unknowing, we find a degree of revelation, experiencing a serenity that leads to expanded understanding, as we realize redemptive action on the Path of Color. O Lord, pour upon man thy spirit and vision of the seeker.

EMILY ROSEBROUGH I recall having a very full, meaningful experience in this temple. I remember how beautiful the scene was, how incredibly spiritual the atmosphere was. I remember seeing a beautiful color of rosy peach, the color of gratitude, and being told by a heavenly guide something about when I return next time, I should bring "the gift" with me. But I didn't know what gift this referred to.

GLENN Might this have something to do with the gift of life?

WILLARD I thought that, too – the gift of life.

MARGARET Because Emily saw rose peach, the color of gratitude, it could be a gentle nudge to become more grateful ... grateful for the gift of life.

MIRIAM WILLIS Gratitude is the 9th Ray in the Spiritual Arc of Purple. The meaning of this ray of gratitude is more than thankfulness. Gratitude is rich, heartfelt, overflowing, loving appreciation. We need to say thank you for everything that comes.

MARY Saying "thank you" creates the most beautiful color. It's the color of henna with rose, patches of orange, pale rosy peach and pale pinks running through. I think saying "thank you" is such a beautiful word. If we say it every day to our brother, our sister, those we live with, after a little while we're saying it to God, because we've grown in appreciation, the very chemistry of our thinking has changed, and we're truly thankful. We do take things for granted. We do tend to make ourselves number one, ignoring so many obvious things.

JUDITH PORTER We know that sometimes a message received from that other world is crystal clear, while other times it gets scrambled when you bring it back to Earth consciousness. But Emily's experience of the gift was quite explicit, wasn't it?

MARY Life is a gift from God, to appreciate and love, for a grateful heart is the mainspring of happiness and is found together with a contented mind. Happiness is a perfume. You can't pour it on others without getting a few drops on yourself. Happiness is to the soul what health is to the body – a healing power. God Bless you, dear ones.

*****

TEMPLE OF ILLUMINATION

MIRIAM From the Area of Selflessness and the Temple of the Seeker, we receive purifying of motives and aspirations that enable us to approach the Temple of Illumination.

Poised on a high hill, the Temple of Illumination shines in luminous glory above a vast area of loveliness which seems to surround it unto infinitude. Like so many hills we encounter in our night work on the Planes, this hill is steep, and one finds as he climbs, the necessity of discarding any weight that might encumber him. Self doubt and fear are two related burdens among the worst, and they seem to cling more closely, threatening to invade one's inner sanctum and destroy his peace. The challenge of this realization causes one to cry for faith, and he finds himself standing on a platform the color of the royal purple of faith, the 2nd ray of the Spiritual Arc of Purple.

Directly in front is a deep chasm of moving light, shimmering in the lettuce green color of selflessness and the yellow of illumination. He must step forward into this abyss, trusting the narrow platform of faith on which he stands. As he takes one step forward he finds that like an escalator, his platform of faith moves with him, sustaining him in perfect balance.

The divine life invading the Channel of his surrendered response floods with new vitality every faculty in an ecstasy of joy and wonder. As a partaker of the divine nature within, his soul emerges from separation—from all darkness of mind and loneliness of heart into the realm of light in another form, another glory, another power, the kingdom of reality. The seeker's eyes are open to its clear illumination, ablaze with God.

Each neophyte trying for admittance to the Temple of Illumination is tested in stability, serenity, relaxation, patience, alertness, and discipline. The neophyte is aware when he hasn't fully passed these tests. He also realizes how fortunate he has been to be taken to the temple and gives thanks.

VIOLET In the Second Chamber in the Temple of Illumination, I thrilled to see jeweled incrustations like crystals. The whole interior was filled with these sparkling jets of light. They protruded from the walls all the way up in bracketed groups. The floor was of white marble which caught the twinkling pots of light and reflected them, so that the whole place seemed alive with tiny lights.

I was conscious of color over our heads, of stripes or bands in many shades of rose, blue, green and yellow, radiating from the crystals. There was a beauty and quiet dignity in this temple quite unlike anything I had experienced before. Somehow it had a deeper solemnity. A feeling here was of a creative force that impregnated our consciousness and made us aware of divinity. An intense sense of wonder entered our perception, and we felt gratitude to the great Creator of such beauty, so we gave thanks, each one expressing it in their own way. There was no sound, only profound silence, but we all felt we had received a blessing and a benediction.

MARY In the 9th Plane Temple of Illumination, we heard these words spoken: "You are entering the Plane of Illumination." Jesus— the perfect example of Illumination. The earliest written, and probably the most authentic account of the illumination of Jesus is: "And straightway, coming up out of the water, he saw the heavens rent asunder, and the spirit of a dove descending upon Him, and a voice came out of the heavens, saying, 'This is my beloved son, in whom I am well pleased.'"

As one's eyes are opened to the radiance of the path of illumination, the standard is distinctly changed when the seeker realizes he must go forth after forty days in the wilderness of soul searching. For only by faith can his vision hold his balance. Ever after an experience of divine love, man realizes he must seek silence, and eventually spiritual rebirth is followed by illumination.

As we enter the lighted path leading to the Temple of Illumination, we behold before us wonderful phenomena of life – soul, spirit, and an overpowering mind consciousness of our oneness with God, the mysteries of immortality and pure spiritual existence. We stand in awe, gazing at the grandeur and beauty of this temple flanked by magnificent terraces with wells of precious stones and gates of jade carved in superlative beauty on the four sides of a vast mountain. Many buildings of glass and pure gold face parks and wide avenues through which run the crystal waters of the River of Life. On either side of that river are the ever-blooming groves of the trees of life bearing all kinds of fruit, whose leaves are for the healing of all nations of God's world.

VIOLET We mount to the height on the stairway of illumination and penetrate still more deeply in the desire to uncover any stumbling block that may be hidden in our inner self that's a bottleneck to progress. A vortex of infinite power extends over the face of the Earth unto salvation and protection. We're reminded of the repeated tests we undergo on our way to fulfilling experiences within the Temple of Illumination.

We open our eyes and see that upon the foundation of ancient wisdom, an edifice of rare dimensions is being built. Illumination is the radiation, the fruit of light and its perfume. Our prayers extend outward, potent and real. We see in our minds the power of God as that great vortex reaching down to people, who in turn reach up in adoration. Earth is caught up into the greatness or Heaven, as a drop of water is absorbed in the ocean.

MARY Revealed to the seeker in this Temple of Illumination is the truth that love is cosmic energy flowing silently and harmoniously to a higher source and back again, just as the clock ball swings from side to side. Love flows from God. It is the thinking of God in the central portion of his universe. Love is faith in action. It's the fruit of a sincere and sacred effort made by the seeker climbing toward the light. These are the things the seeker has laid down: sorrow, doubt and confusion. Things he has taken up are universal love and understanding.

The seeker's soul goes forth as a young eagle in early morning. Its wings and the rose-kiss of morn upon its crest are unfettered, freed for the heights. He knows Jesus Christ has bridged the chasm between man and God, and that following him, we can't lose our way. Spiritual illumination comes to all who earn its light. Only when man's spiritual perception is unfolded and he attains divine knowledge of self will he know the Voice and obey only the noblest demands of spirit, making himself a vehicle for the expression of Divine Will.

MIRIAM WILLIS As the wheel of life turns, in the absence of understanding, our tests become more severe, but as we learn, our tests are welcome and joyful experiences.

MARY Only when the soul is awakened can we understand what is given in the higher light, as we're seeking soul illumination, so that all of our outward expressions shall be as perfect as our true selves. Illumination comes from within. Truth has many facets, but the jewel in the lotus is always the same.

SYLVIA Where would we place the Tower of Illumination?

MIRIAM WILLIS The Tower is in the Temple.

MARY Do you remember how we go in? There's the great tower in front of us. We walk through gates and descend into a lovely garden. The flowers are unusually beautiful. Water sounds like bells. We walk on, we climb this Tower. I think you'll find you went up a circular staircase.

LOLA I received another part of the Tower tonight. It was translucent. Within it I saw the cross, or it became a cross, because on the sides of the Tower, the light emanated out into the arms of the cross, then I was able to see the light forming the rest of the cross through the whole Tower.

MARY That's fine. We have two people here who've been in the same spot this week. You were in a part of the Temple of Illumination, a part that's of the illumination of worship. You were at the Tower side.

LOLA Tower of Illumination in the Temple of Illumination?

MARY Yes. We're privileged to experience the tests and receive the benefits of enlightened insight, wisdom and love which is part of the 9th Plane Temple of Illumination. These opportunities are offered many times, for illumination is gained only by seeking to know and to overcome the natural traits of selfishness and self-centeredness, through union with God.

LOLA In meditation I asked if I could see a temple that I had recently visited, and I was given a very interesting structure. My attention was drawn to the upper part, the Tower. This was more oval in shape, I believe, unless there was a higher, more pointed structure in a larger section.

The center section I was observing began to open up almost like a lotus, and a section of it almost like a petal, began to come forward and go over the lower part. As it came down, it revealed this almost like a jewel inner part that had many facets like a jewel would – cut back here and there, and so it had great depth as well. It seemed more of the rays were radiating out, more the blues and purples. I got the words, "See and seen through a glass darkly." I got the impression that there were eight sides to it.

MARY Yes. Now what you were really seeing was the Hindu expression of the Temple of Illumination, the Tower of Illumination.

We experience tests and receive the benefits of enlightened insight, wisdom and love which this part of the 9th Plane offers many times. For illumination is gained only by seeking to know and to overcome the natural traits of doubt and self centeredness through union with God.

Illumination is a gift of God. Through service we give as a gift to others, illumination is given us, and it's truly a gift we receive. I never say you have to sacrifice, but I do say you have to put someone before yourself. A great part of love is first thinking of others above yourself. It can be very difficult.

LOLA With regard to "through a glass darkly," I feel very strongly this could refer to the mirrors we see on the Other Side. It makes sense that over there, we see things as they really are, "face to face." For the time we're over there in our night work, our spiritual reception, so to speak, is heightened, we do see "face to face," we're deeply impressed, and a portion of that energy is imbued in us. We retain a portion of it. But after we die and the Other Side becomes our home, we will really see "face to face." We will understand far better, more thoroughly, after we've made our transition, when we live over there.

JOHN BRANCHFLOWER Does the 9th Plane Temple of Illumination take up all of the top of the hill?

MARY No, it doesn't. It's built strangely. It's more than a hill; it's a mountain. And some of it is rock hewn; you go to what we'd call the gates of the temple. There are gates on all sides, but should you come up the rear way, which you can do walking around this mountain, when you come up there, you see that this part is for the more primitive people of the Earth. Primitive men knew illumination differently than we do, in that they stressed fire, water, sound – it's sensing rather than intuition. Primitive man had as great a faith in God as we have. But it's a fire god that has to protect him, so in the temple, he's shown fire.

You look up to the rear of this great temple – I call it the rear because it caters to the least developed people in evolution. You'll see these people plodding up that mountain with a great deal more strength than we know anything about, and looking up at that fire. The heavens will just be alight with that fire. By and by, there's a silver glow that descends over all. And no matter what primitive race you find, they start in on their own worship, and they praise God. So God is naturally in the life, in the heart of every human being, even though they don't know how to explain it. But these primitives express it with a great deal of force.

And then nearly all of them, in worshipful thankfulness, break down some rocks. They go to this great rocky ledge, they create these flint-like holes, they go into that rock, and perhaps right in the heart of the rock, someone discovers opals or some other precious stone or gorgeous color. Then they go through gyrations of a dance and worship the Most High, because he has given them the gem, you see, the color, the light; he has welcomed them with a gift.

They leave the gift there. Therefore, many walls are studded with gifts that those far back in the law of evolution have created – the gift for us to see in those temples. I think that has gone down through the ages! They said that 20,000 years ago a tribe created these jeweled windows. So the evolution of the human soul speaks strongly to me of why we should expect incarnation and reincarnation. Because we see the soul that has moved up, and up and up in the scheme of things, always looking toward the light, toward the illuminated light of God's love.

WILLARD In terms of reincarnation, maybe we in this class were once incarnated as those primitive people you speak of. We – or some of us, anyway – might have been among those who carved from stone 20,000 years ago.

MARY Instead of a universal illumination, though it is that – this is a personal application of illumination. Look calmly and with confidence, knowing that the penetrating ray cleanses and heals as it reveals. Then leave the growth and the fruitage to the Father. Stand erect as you ascend, knowing each step on this stairway is a rock of salvation. There are the slow times and the dull times, but remember, his light and love change not.

MIRIAM WILLIS We need varying degrees of discipline on this stairway of life, and it takes a deal of climbing. But let patience have her perfect work that Christ be formed within and shine out in brilliant radiance to bless and guide.

******

REVIEW VII
MORE ABOUT COLOR

The Color Path is a mystical journey toward development of the soul, a way of illumination and intuitive perception.

Color is a measurable vibration in the electromagnetic spectrum, expressing matter moving at varying speeds and densities.

Color rays embodying both positive and negative qualities are used in spiritual development and healing. Healing with color is an ancient art that has been used throughout the ages. According to records, Egyptians, Essenes, Greeks, Buddhists, Hebrews, Persians and Tibetans all used color for therapeutic purposes. The Greek city of Heliopolis, City of the Sun, was renowned for its healing temples, where sunlight was broken up into individual colors, each one used to treat particular conditions. Jesus, according to esoteric records, is said to have studied there.

All of us are influenced by color, whether consciously or subliminally. Man lives in a universe powerfully designed by color, whose energy is both visible and invisible. We live in two worlds, and color occupies both, each in its unique way. We explore color at both levels, with emphasis on the invisible world, which becomes visible when our higher senses are attuned. In the invisible world are many octaves of light. Just as each color has its own individual wave length, so each has a message and a special effect.

We can "throw" color on people or on ourselves to become more balanced human beings. We can refine and balance our chakras with daily use of the Color Channel of Our Being. We use the Channel in prayer and for meditation and to get answers to questions. Color is the starting point of a journey toward inner purification. It's a gentle way to develop spiritually that eases the path and helps one's growth and ongoing. Using Color can create changes in people and conditions that bring them into balance.

Color is a living ray that operates all about you that builds within you a creative energy that you've not had before. Color is light revealed—vibration, energy, the visible essence of the life force. The Color path is a mystical journey toward soul development. Color bridges the physical dimension with the higher dimensions. It is safe, and it protects. Color develops intuition. It is a catalyst, a change agent. It has the power to be used in self therapy and soul expansion for healing oneself and others. With color, we can dissolve negatives and create positives.

Color points the way to greater understanding of oneself and others. It can be used to convey meaning between ourselves and the Creator and between the ego and the inner self. If we have workplace, family or financial problems, Color provides help to work things out. Color will keep you balanced, improve your health, contribute to your success and happiness. Color establishes harmonious relationships. Color prayer removes mental strain. It takes away difficult emotions that accompany the heavy vibration of a sick body. The study and practice of Creative Color causes expansion of consciousness to experience spiritual sensing. Colors are spiritual food. The more we climb the ladder of color, the more we grow.

"Creative Color Analysis" is a lifetime study, a matchless spiritual and practical aid toward spiritual development. Those who wish to learn more about Mary's Color teaching may wish to consult previous books in the Planes of Heaven series, particularly the second volume, *Everything You Always Wanted to Know about Heaven But Didn't Know Where to Ask*, as well as the book *Creative Color Analysis*, by Mary and students, available online at http://www.creativecolor.org.

******

> SIXTH STEEP - To the AREA and TEMPLE OF EXPANSION, TEMPLE OF REVERENCE, TEMPLE OF LIFE, and TEMPLE OF AWAKENING
>
> First Station: SELF ALIGNMENT This is a gathering of one's forces by magnetic attraction so that each quality contributes to the other in harmonious order.
>
> Second Station: SELF CONTAINMENT. This establishes a recognition of the reservoir of supply and is the fruit of one's aligned forces.
>
> Third Station: ENJOYMENT of ONESELF To enjoy one's self is to be at peace with God and man in thankful recognition of re-creative life energy, always available.
>
> Fourth Station: SELF CONTROL. This is maintained through the balanced forces developed to maturity. Disciplined action.
>
> Fifth Station: SELF EFFACEMENT. This requires humility; the yielding of the personal ego to the purification of desirelessness that enables one to function freely at all levels.
>
> Sixth Station: POISE Poise is the fruit of balanced forces operating in the life.

*****

We've been traveling on these power lines, experiencing six Stations on the Steep for the tests we go through. We now come into the Area of Expansion and over to the Temple of Reverence, Temple of Life and the Temple of Awakening.

AREA AND TEMPLE OF EXPANSION

After many tests along the Eightfold Path, ever lured onward, upward and beyond, the seeker enters the 9th Plane of Expansion, desiring to be identified with greater understanding than he has known. The vastness without now seems to be within. He becomes identified with spiritual qualities that expand his consciousness, integrating purifying elements with the higher refinement of spirit, until the light and vitality generated becomes illuminated wisdom guiding into all truth, tempering his thoughts, words and deeds with an increasing action of maturity, while seeing the light of God in self and in his brother. From this point on, life becomes his accepted destiny. He walks in radiance with a listening ear and quickened response to his guiding light that fails not, so long as he keeps within its protection.

MARY On a wall in a shrine of worship, we beheld these words: "The soul of man is immortal, and its future growth and splendor has no limit."

We spent many hours of training in the Area of Expansion. The teacher of wisdom came to us and said, "Wait patiently for the ripeness of understanding. Your mind must become as a placid pool in which to see your real self. Close your eyes to the seeming, and follow the light within. When illumination touches the heart, man goes within himself to the Book of Life."

In times of need, a seer appears who has dipped his pen in the stream of reality, and the flame from his mind afire lures the soul to awareness. "You think man a strange creature, for you see only the case that holds the jewel," he says. "If a man is asleep, what matters a sunset? Man sleeps within a pit of his own digging, living in the shade, weaving days into years. But man evolved is a seeker, and when the light shines in his heart, the seeker sees God in man. Life urges him to walk on through the shadows, open the eyes of his soul and read in every mountain peak, on each foam-capped wave, God's spoken word."

MIRIAM WILLIS The climb toward the Temple of Expansion is steep, the attraction strongly magnetic, luring one through ephemeral vagueness in faith and hope to clearer fulfillment. One's powers are tested here, and the muscles of the soul are strengthened thereby. This climb is also joyous – full of song and laughter dappled with the sunlight of illumination and the cool shade of quiet resting places.

One glimpses the Temple of Expansion on the crest of a thick tree-clad hill, appearing as a sunrise heralding the dawn. It towers high above, surrounded by a multitude of fragrant flowers, watered by cool fountains, splashing waterfalls and streamlets of pale blue water. The temple itself is so ablaze with light one wonders whether this emanates from within or is the reflection of the rising sun. We are attracted to investigate.

The temple appears to be posited in the grey-green Psychological color of basic understanding, of variegated marble shot through with the nile green color of awareness, the 9th ray of the Spiritual Arc of Green. It's surrounded by many lancet turrets of great height. The colors above the nile green are the pale lettuce green of desirelessness, gradually changing to warmer tints of yellow, peach, rose, blue, lavender and many pastel tints of light moving on into seeming infinitude.

The entrances are intricately carved in a pattern resembling intricate lace, with each entrance guarded by an angel of light. As one enters the Temple of Expansion, one is filled with an almost floating sensation of weightlessness. Within, the atmosphere is delicately fragrant. It looks like the temple has no roof – in fact, no enclosure, just great expansion. One feels an identification with this expansion, a power which no materiality can limit, for its light and substance passes through one, so refined is its essence, so powerful its gentleness and so secure its balance. This initiation is a preparation for the further reaches of experience.

The angelic hosts were gathered. The air was vibrant with harmony. Life's sonata flows through all forms, in the magic musical tones of rhythm, in unfathomable speech leading to the infinite. God is the source of all life. Knowing this, we climb on to a higher vision, for vision is intuitional awakening.

HELEN DECANT I brought back some impressions: I saw a temple that was all alabaster set with pearls. The trees surrounding it are very old, with lots of moss hanging like in the deep South. Inside the temple, there was scarcely an aisle without crowds of people, yet despite the milling crowds all over, harmony prevailed. I was aware of a cloud of rose lavender, then blue, where our teachers come to speak. Every word they spoke seemed to be a pearl of wisdom, and we dropped to our knees to acknowledge them. You could almost taste the beauty.

There are many pillars and a pool in this temple. I was particularly aware of the color of harmony, the grey-pink-lavender , 8th ray of the Spiritual Arc of Purple, and of the pink lavender color of inspiration.

BILL JACKSON   I was told that in the Temple of Expansion, each person receives the elements he particularly needs, much as a seed draws to itself the elements in the soil that nurture it to maturity.

MARGARET   I brought back a lesson or message, first about how to get rid of worry and fear, and how those keep us from abundant living. Secondly, how to take in more of the life force through not thinking so much of the physical body, but expanding — taking appropriate colors into the aura, thus getting to feel fluidic.

MARY   We incorporate all that, you know, into a fluidic force that flows around you. So when worry attacks, you reach out. In other words, you plug in and creative energy will relieve you of anxiety. I know that you can overcome fear that way.

MARGARET   It was interesting how to take it in through the aura.

MARY   That's what it's for.

SYLVIA   I had a fire test in which I was given two sets of matches, both of which had my name on them. I was told to choose which type of matches to use to start the fire for my test. One was a match book, the other a box of matches. I can't remember which one I selected, but I do recall a fire started that soon was blazing, burning very high and wide. Despite initial fear, I walked through the fire without incident. I did not burn; my fear dissolved, I felt nothing threatening; even the intense heat didn't bother me. I emerged feeling from that fire as if I'd made a major step forward by passing this test.

MARY As indeed you did.

JANE WRIGHT I guess fire tests were the order of the day (or should I say night), because I had one too. Mine was different, though. Mine was a vivid reenactment of something that happened when I was six years old, when my four year old cousin and I inadvertently started a fire in our neighborhood. We wanted to toast marshmallows and didn't know anything about making a fire. We found some matches my parents had hidden in a drawer. We had no idea what we were doing! We were so scared when the fire we unintentionally started began spreading like crazy all over the field we were in behind my parents' house, and the fire department raced with loud bells clanging to extinguish it. I have harbored a lot of guilt over that incident my entire life, being the cause of that fire. Strangely, the fire test I had on the Other Side this week eased my guilt – I'm not sure how, but it absolutely did.

MARY You learned that we're accountable for everything from the age of seven on. You weren't seven yet; you were six. You realized you don't have to account for this incident. You were too young to know any better. Finding this out relieved your conscience.

PATTI And her cousin was only four!

LOLA I recall something I believe was also a test, but of a different kind. I brought back from the other night's work the encountering of people I didn't recognize, but to whom I was indebted. I stood with hands outstretched in worship and gratitude. People came before me that I should have remembered for thoughtful, caring things they'd done for me. They were people who'd been injured in the war. They were hospital cases. One after the other, they were brought before me, and I was giving thanks for these people. I thought maybe this was a type of test?

MARY That's a type of test you get! Then, when you're standing there and the music picks you up and you find yourself in rhythm with the thoughts around you, there are many things you'd love to remember that you haven't the capacity to remember. But you're building power. It's within you; you're entering into the very bloodstream of your physical life, storing energy to remember these things.

JOHN BASINSKI You say you "haven't the capacity to remember." So then how can we learn to remember? What extra is needed? And how do we come by it?

MARY You have to put forth the energy. Best time is when you wake in the morning. And before, during and after meditation. You get into it not because you think it's a duty, but because you really want to get at it, and it seems that nothing goes right if you don't keep that tryst. Man needs to truly believe in the expansion of consciousness he has received in the Temple of Expansion where he's been in training. There he was told to overcome the human habit of thinking fearful and negative thoughts, eventually to progress into the realm of reverence. He must honor and respect himself. Self unfoldment comes to man when he lives in the wisdom of profound respect mingled with love, exalting life in faith.

*****

TEMPLE OF REVERENCE

MARY When the seeker glimpses the vastness yet to be attained, his soul is filled with gratitude and cries out for expression, leading him on to the Temple of Reverence. As he descends through a grotto of darkness, his faith is rewarded by increasing light revealing things that grow within the earth and the sea.

Traveling onward into brilliant opaline blue becoming mother of pearl, in the midst of this beautiful color, he sees a magnificent temple reaching to highest heaven. He becomes conscious of a great company of angels and is transfixed by the beauty and holy stillness.

A harmonious hum, as though all nature sings, issues forward. As he joins in this, he becomes aware of an upsurge of reverent praise rising from within all things in adoration and wonder. He realizes that he and all living things are like musical instruments, that reverence awakened in the soul recognizes and shares – for the music emanates through each being until the whole of creation is singing praise for all life in reverent adoration of the great Creator indwelling and surrounding all.

MIRIAM WILLIS Not only does the necessity for testings penetrate the seeker's consciousness, but also the privilege of such opportunities fills his soul with awe and reverence.

MARY I want to ask you, what is the color of wisdom? There are people who don't know the color.

MARGARET Well, the color of spiritual wisdom is a beautiful, deep red plum, almost a reddish purple. That brings me to a question ... I'd like to ask about a couple of things I saw this week. First, there was mostly that red plum color of spiritual wisdom; then I saw an altar. The backdrop was an arch in all in shades of the Spiritual Arc of Purple, from deepest purple to palest lavender, with a brilliant cross in the middle with a symmetrical lily pattern. And then there was a dome made of large strips, centered at the middle. And rainbows – not ordinary ones, but different colored rainbows around and at the center of the temple dome. Movement subsided, and there was a shaft of light in greens and lavenders. Were those any place we've been this week?

MARY Yes, it's the Temple of Reverence.

MIRIAM WILLIS Spiritual wisdom, the 5th Ray of the Spiritual Arc of Purple that Margaret speaks of, is particularly lovely. It has a rose-orange underglow that combines desire with love and lifts it to a higher plane. It contains as well the colors of faith, love and peace at the Earth level. Here is timeless wisdom intelligently applied. It's the wisdom one expects to hear from a great spiritual teacher. It comes from a height and therefore has an elevated perspective on all factors involved in any problem. It suggests good solutions to benefit all concerned.

HELEN von GEHR I had a picture of water. Rising up out of it was a maiden in a reverent position, like a Buddha, and above her head was a lovely large lotus blossom. I understood that it's out of the depths that wisdom comes.

MARY That's right. This Temple of Reverence takes a great deal of the symbolism of India. You saw the lotus; the lotus has eight petals, and the pistons and stamens are jeweled. Those leaves form a protective roof. It's a perfectly remarkable sight.

HANK It seems to me that a great deal of the 9th Plane has symbols of India, for instance the lotus that Helen just mentioned. And also haven't we seen more angels on this plane than in the previous planes?

MIRIAM WILLIS That's very true of the 9th Plane. Now, what we're going to consider is so much beyond what the mental mind is able to register. Try to recall. See whether anything rings a bell with something you've brought back from your night sojourns in these wonderful temples and areas we're privileged to go to at night. So let us just ask the blessed spirit to open us, and then if you feel a chord of response toward your memory or inner response to your sensing, try to latch hold of it.

DAN I was very aware in this temple of the Eightfold Path we're treading, and how we lead many lives to arrive at knowledge of our true selves.

MICHAEL I also had that awareness of being exposed to deeper truths of our journey on the Eightfold Path. I heard a lecture in this temple, fortifying my awareness that for thousands of years, the Hindus have told us that Atman – the true self — is eternal, and that man's spiritual development occurs in many lifetimes, during which we pursue various directions on our way to becoming masters.

The Hindus tell us there are four possible aims to human life, known as the Purusharthas, that we can take. These aims are: Kama (desire, love and pleasure); Artha (wealth, prosperity, and glory); Dharma (righteousness, morality, and virtue); and Moksha (liberation from the cycle of reincarnation). Existence is conceived as the progression of the Atman, the soul, during many lifetimes, its ultimate motive being liberation.

DALE That ties in very neatly with what we're trying to accomplish on the steeps and in the heavenly temples.

VIOLET When I woke this morning, I was conscious that when you rise after a night in the temples, there's a holy presence within and without, the feeling or attitude of deep respect tinged with awe and veneration.

RUBY PERKINS I did get an impression of the Temple of Reverence. I had the feeling of being in a large chapel. There was a velvet-like carpet in it. The rows in which the seats were placed were very steep. The scene was quite dark; there was no light, but there was a luminosity. The altar was down lower than the seats, and it was luminous.

VIOLET This is what I learned in the Temple of Reverence: as all the elements of which anything is made are of God, it follows that to be truly reverent, we send forth a love to him and receive back in return a flowing of that love force.

Reverence requires a sense of gentleness and awe. One touches with gentleness anything one is drawn to because of its beauty. All these qualities then, must be implanted in the being that is full of reverence: awe, wonder, worship, gentleness, admiration, love, awareness of beauty. These have become qualities of soul, of eternal value, which means that soul has learned balance. One has been tested to be accepted into the company of those who recognize God in all of his creation, and realize all is sacred and all is part of his plan. Each life now shows forth the fruits of reverence.

The golden color of the 11th Ray of the Spiritual Arc of Yellow flows forth, and the colors of the 11th and 12th Rays of the Spiritual Arc of Red are also those of this Temple.

GRACE HALE That yellow color assumed importance for us before, when we were leaving the Plateau between the 8th and 9th Planes, ready to enter the 9th Plane. Jeanne saw a golden road.

MIRIAM WILLIS That 11th Ray of the Spiritual Arc of Yellow, a rich sun yellow, is a ray of developing action, feeding and stimulating spiritual growth. A person radiating this color in their aura sees the big picture. Just as the sun makes chemical changes in green fruit, bringing it to ripeness, so the rich spiritual sun yellow makes chemical changes in one's nature.

MARY It "ripens" good traits and gives one a new sweetness of character. The separated has become integrated. One now sees and understands the great pattern of life alive within the God-center, Christ Consciousness, and is able to fit into this great pattern. Such a person now truly can bring spiritual expression into daily living. They can see their Earth life in terms of spiritual lessons. Happiness has matured into joy in the soul. This soul has sought through many channels. His nebulous ideas have become synchronized into a force unifying himself with the Christ within.

The 11th ray of the Spiritual Arc of Red, meaning "tenderness and concern for a brother," appears as a light pink, at times seen with an inner glow of yellow bisque. One grows in ability to sense and then to realize many degrees of vibration. With this maturing sensitivity, one feels and knows that God is everywhere and within all that is, comforting and blessing us with this delicate color.

*****

TEMPLE OF LIFE

MIRIAM WILLIS The Temple of Life is located to the right of the Temple of Reverence at the upper part of the Area of Expansion, on the left hand side of the 9th Plane. The whole area is alive with blossoming, breathtaking beauty clothed in the rich verdure of pure unsullied growth. One travels in awe over rolling hills, where flowers sway in the fresh breeze, scattering their fragrance, and where streamlets wind their way to pools that lie near paths the seeker treads.

MARY In the Temple of Life we experience five cleansing pools. These pools provide treatment for conditions in need of healing. We need to bathe in these pools before we can see the Temple of Life.

As one pursues his way, he is attracted to this or that pool by an impelling desire, and as he wades into ever deepening water, an inner realization grows, and he sees qualities that need cleansing, healing, strengthening, changing, or revealing. He swims in each pool, emerging on the other side to find his garments are perfectly dry, shining with purer loveliness. It is as though scales are removed from his eyes, so he can see into the heart of beauty itself.

The Temple of Life rises before us, descending to such a depth as to have no beginning, reaching upward with no ending, revealing all colors like those of a great master's aura.

One enters through his own doorway, which is low and dark. This is an awesome experience. The seeker must feel his way, unseeing, up a spiral which, as it ascends, reflects more and more light and beauty. The path on this spiral of ascent is narrow, and he must watch and travel carefully, pausing to view each revelation life has offered. He feels he has climbed this way many times before, yet there is here a newness of discovery and often of surprise, as he sees life revealed.

Continuing his arduous journey, he experiences every stage of life with a feeling of personal understanding of his own, and a closeness in understanding of his fellow man. Life with all its lights and shadows, its trials and temptations, its failures and successes unfold to him.

As he perseveres, the way becomes lighted and a fatigue which had assailed him now drops away. He reaches a height where many spirals like his own merge into a oneness of joyful understanding. He inhales a delicate perfume, standing with many of his fellow seekers, each clothed like himself in beautiful colors, in a vast chamber of iridescent color. The triumph of winning the challenge of life responds to the great Creator in praise and thanksgiving.

In the Temple of Life, every seeker was told that nothing stands in the way of the search for understanding, for when the seeker begins his search on the material plane, he has brought God's creative energy forward and placed doubt, self criticism, worry, envy, and resentment into the background of his consciousness. It's been proven that a man is literally what he thinks, his character being the complete sum of all his thoughts. Man is made or unmade by himself.

In the armory of thought, he forges the weapons by which he can destroy himself, but he can also fashion the tools with which he builds for himself heavenly mansions of joy and peace. By the right choice and true application of thought, man ascends to the point of illumination, reaching divine perfection.

Of all the beautiful truths given the seeker in the heavenly temples, the great promises pertaining to the soul, none is more gladdening than the divine promise that man is born with the plan of his life inscribed on his soul. May the seeker find understanding, wisdom, and have the power to know brotherhood.

VIOLET Approaching this temple, I saw a fantastically intricate, very delicate lacy screen. We were looking through it. It was apparently carved in some soft stone, and was of beautiful workmanship. This was part of the Temple of Life, and represented life in all its wonder and variety. This is life's emergence, development, glorification and absorption into higher forms. As one experiences the sequence of events, one marvels at the pattern the weaving back and forth to these areas and temples offers the seeker; for the greater the expansion of consciousness, the greater the reverence, and the greater the reverence, the greater is the zest for life and desire to understand and partake of its fullness. Thus the soul is led onward, always at its own pace of unfoldment in the pattern of living.

PATTI A teacher was trying to dramatize a certain point. There were three men who appeared to be Chinese, each wearing long narrow brocade gowns clear to the floor, and identical headdresses. There were two small square pillows, one on top of another.

MARY We were in the Temple of Life when you had that experience. You said "pillows?"

PATTI Yes.

RUBY When Patti mentioned the pillows, it reminded me of seeing a bride's pillow, real fancy, with lace around it and beautiful jewels. I thought it was the pearl of great price, but perhaps it has some other meaning.

MARY I think you have it. It was a satin pillow?

RUBY Yes.

MARY Yes, pearl of great price. I tell you, dears, if we go back in history – I can go back 5,000 years and present the "pillow" to you. Kings are crowned; their crowns are carried on pillows all the way through history. And in our churches – the wedding; the kneeling pillow at the kneeling bench; and the pillows to sit on.

Besides that, there is nearly always a padded pillow for the Great Book to lie upon. Pillows are symbolic of softening the message—to take away the Earth influence, and let the message come through to the outer pillow—soften. So the "pillow" is a softener.

PATTI I'm sorry to say that I had a small hatchet and was going to chop down a very small pine tree about three feet tall that had very long needles. Ultimately, I didn't.

VIOLET Well, maybe you inadvertently took some of the needles out of someone's consciousness and helped, whether you used the hatchet or not. You know, criticism, many times, is "needling."

MARY We come into the world, and what one man might call karma another man might say a load of guilt, another man might say, God gives us our sorrows to bear or a load to carry. The indication of being able to live this life and share through faith – pillows are placed in front of the altar; man makes any gift he wishes to give, and many times a great philanthropy appears in the world.

Somebody is moved to give of their substance. They don't know why, but they'll say, "I was moved to do this." Our first orthopedic hospital in the country grew out of a condition like that. The man was a church member, but not the kind of Christian that would part with money. And he had this vision of taking his gold and putting it on himself, wearing it. As he told it, a Hindu prophet talked to him along the way to a temple, and he changed; he gave of his substance, and our first orthopedic hospital was founded.

PATTI Is there a symbolism behind all three men in my vision giving pillows?

MARY The pillow is a place to put your head when you're tired. The Christ Child was born in a manger. He had no place to lay his head. Now what is sleep? Sleep is the removal from Earth thoughts, being out of the body, and our training comes through that time of night. Therefore, the pillow – or the covering, the covers, the blankets.

And you know, as we look back into all Biblical things, you remember the blankets that were woven, the shawls? Everyone was protected with a shawl; accordingly, astrologically, it was the color that belonged to the person. The astrologers in those days – whether it was psychological or whatever – they worked wonders with the people. They would give away old shawls so that the poor, who had no covers, would be provided. They would bring the poor into the temples, and make sure people who had more than enough would give their blankets to the poor.

MARGARET I had another picture last week, seeing a round, small tower with a low-peaked roof. It was colored a soft green; it had a single low door in it with an enormous key right in the center. And I was to turn the door and go in. I had to stoop to get in. Once inside, there were just one arch after another of beautiful soft greens of understanding.

MARY That's our Temple of Life, dear.

ESTHER BARNES Mary, why would one see silhouettes as though through a silk screen?

MARY It's often seeing through the Channel. You don't always see color first, and you don't always see things life size. You may see them small and silhouettes at first. That's the growth of seeing.

*****

TEMPLE OF AWAKENING

FRED Awakening is an important part of the Eightfold Path we've been following since the 8th Plane, and now on the 9th Plane.

MICHAEL In the spiritual traditions of India, consciousness is understood to be obscured by defilements which are compared to clouds covering the sun. These defilements are accumulations in the unconscious caused by past actions. Because of them, what one perceives as reality is a picture of the world filtered through one's unconscious conditioning. The goal is to awaken and adjust to this, to dissolve delusion to effect transformation. Enlightenment enables us to see reality as it is, rather than through the veils of Maya. Enlightenment brings one into Christ Consciousness or Nirvana.

MIRIAM WILLIS In the Temple of Awakening, we're particularly aware that to awaken is the real purpose of living on Earth, to expand our awareness. The Fifth Ray of the Spiritual Arc of Blue, a deep green-blue Copenhagen blue, is an energized emotional force that activates sensitivity. The meaning encompasses feeling rather than reason, awakened intuition. We're also aware of the Fifth Spiritual Ray of the Arc of Green, green-yellow with an old rose midray, which opens us to the vibrant universal force that is entering our consciousness, making us more flexible and open-minded, bringing expanded perception and flexibility.

FRANK I was aware this week of a greater understanding of the meaning of awakening, and how on the Eightfold Path, awakening means a change of heart, awareness and mindfulness.

JOHN BASINSKI Awakening is waking up to the true nature of reality, to our Buddha nature, to Christ Consciousness, to beyond previous limitations.

GLENN In the Temple of Awakening we learned that in all tests, love is the answer. In this temple the soul truly grows. It's like the dawning of a beautiful sunrise whose flame enters the soul. Henceforth that flame of inner joy burns at a constant glory, reverence and worship, and is never extinguished.

MIRIAM WILLIS We spent most of our training hours in this temple. We were made aware of our responsibility to our world. We were told gladness springs from the spirit of God. We were told of Christ's life, the great revelation of how the wealth of spirit was given one who had gained an understanding heart. All men must overcome to gain development. Do not resist the healing guidance of the Path. Ask God each day for an understanding heart.

MARY JEAN COPE I had the feeling we were tested much more than previously, that the tests in this temple were extremely challenging and literally endless.

MIRIAM Yes, indeed.

GENE HAFNER What particular tests did we undergo here?

MARY We were tested on sharing, self control, self realization, vanities, growth, grace, and faith.

CAROL I recall a water test in this temple. I was immersed in the middle of a large body of water, presumably an ocean. I was aware, even in that vast ocean, that my toenails were painted bright red, which struck me as odd because I have never painted my toenails. I heard the name Costa Rica, and assumed I was swimming off the coast of that country, the translation of which is "rich coast," the name which no doubt contains a message.

The whole point of this water test is that I was to help a pig whose mouth was painted the same identical red color as my toenails! A peculiar facet of my wearing toenail polish in the test is that I'm the only member of my family who doesn't paint their toenails. Mother, aunts, grandmothers, sisters and cousins all do or did – everybody but me. I've never liked nail polish; in fact, I really dislike it. I think Costa Rica, rich coast, is a positive message ... like telling me I'm in a good place in life – which I definitely believe I am! The red color, despite my antipathy toward nail polish, was nevertheless a positive, energizing me. And as for the pig, I take that as a positive, too, because I do like pigs a lot. I think they make lovely pets, although I don't have one myself. But that test did a lot for me. I wish I could describe how liberated I feel since that experience.

ESTHER ESTABROOK I find it so interesting about the nail polish. She dislikes nail polish. To me, this test must have to do with the likes and dislikes that we face on the Eightfold Path.

GEORGE And that we have to overcome.

HANK Could you say something more about the different type of tests we have over there?

MARY The tests we're given on each plane are always designed to meet the need of the individual. Both the tests we face there and the ones we face here, we account for there. You're given fire, water and air tests: the fire tests deal with physical purification; water tests purify the emotional body; and the mental body is cleaned in air tests. There is specific testing and development in each temple.

VIOLET And afterwards, we'll always have an Earth test to match.

MARGARET It's interesting to identify the Earth tests, to recognize them when they pop up, understand what they relate to from the test we had on the Other Side.

JUNE WALTERS How would you interpret a water test, what they do for us?

MARY In a water test, water would be around you in some way. You might be struggling against a current, trying to stay afloat, feel you're drowning, be caught in heavy rainfall, anything to do with water. Usually the water test makes you remember things you ought not to forget. At night we're released from the subconscious darkness, from the hold these things have on our minds.

And the water test also removes doubt, clears us of any doubt we're carrying around. We're released from subconscious darkness, from the hold these things have on our minds.

We call it a water test because the test is for fear, and fear has to be taken out. We're certainly fearful. The water comes up to our chin, and our feet aren't touching anything to hold us. Many say the test was like drowning. All of a sudden the water seems to envelop you. In that moment we're under the water, and when we come up, it's like we have never lived before. You know who you are. A water test is a cleansing. It's a breaking of old molds of thinking. There's a clean, new mold starting again, a beginning. It's a great change; you come back purified.

IDA I had both a water and a fire test together. It was a very difficult test, as if I were wrestling with my very soul. I was supposed to be taking care of an infant named Timothy for his parents. We were in a row boat on a body of salt water. Baby Timothy was in a bassinette, and I was sitting a few feet behind, watching him. I'm confused about the exact details that ensued, not sure of what went wrong or how, but it apparently involved carelessness on my part, something I either did or did not do, one fatal mistake that led to a terrible tragedy. I think maybe I hadn't covered little Timothy with his blanket quite properly, that I left a small part of him exposed, which for some reason caused his torso to open up, be vulnerable to the elements and to start bleeding. Smelling blood, a shark appeared and sank his teeth into the baby. Suddenly, the baby was consumed by flames that burned him alive until there was nothing at all left of him. Seeing his ashes blowing away in the wind, I felt agonizingly terrible remorse for whatever it was I had done or not done.

My most urgent thought was: what can I possibly tell Baby Timothy's parents? The precious child they had entrusted to my care was gone, not a trace left of him – because of my neglect, my carelessness. This test caused me to reflect on my childhood, when my mother was always admonishing me, "You're so careless!" Her criticism worried me, because I felt I had no control over that failing, that my carelessness was unintentional; I just had no insight about what made me be this way or how I could change. I couldn't help myself!

You might think I woke with a negative feeling after this wrenching temple test, but no, I woke feeling enlightened and relieved. It was as if a burden had been lifted.

MARY You and Mother had your differences when you were growing up. Mother has been on the Other Side for a number of years now, having had much time to reflect on your relationship. She's happy to see you, so the two of you are able to resolve issues that came between you when you were young. You've made progress, and you did pass a very difficult test, hence your feeling a burden was lifted. Did you know the meaning of the name "Timothy" means "honoring God?" You might think on that, too.

ESTHER BARNES The fact that the child Timothy died because of Carol's carelessness could be a message about honoring God, then.

NITA In my night work experience in this temple, I discovered I had left a book bag containing important notebooks and personal files at what seemed like a school, a library, or a public meeting place. It was several hours later that I made this worrisome discovery of loss of something absolutely essential to my existence. I was concerned that someone else would access my private information and I would lose all my work and the irreplaceable files I needed for my personal records. I went back to look for the book bag and found it was still there; no one had stolen it. I was so relieved! However, this incident was a warning to me that I need to be more attentive and – like Carol, less careless!

MARGARET Did we all have to deal with carelessness this week? Because I felt I had a lesson in that, too.

MARY That's right.

HANK Did we all pass our tests, or did some fail? Because I felt like I failed.

MARY You'll know when you fail a test. In many temples, a cup of nectar is offered. Whether we receive it or not depends on our reaction to the particular tests in that temple. If we don't pass the test, we don't receive the cup. You know through the vibratory activity of your being whether you receive it or not. We can stand there and someone else can be drinking that nectar, we want it so bad we can just taste it, but then, sometimes it's quite bitter because we've failed to be able to take the cup, through anger, through little apologies that seem to upset us and offset us at times. We all go through that loss of not being able to take the cup of nectar that's offered. No one comments, because a person wouldn't dare comment. You might be the next fellow not to receive that cup.

What have you done today? What has this day meant to you? Have you even thought of the temple where you're going tonight? Have you thought of the beauty of it and the lasting force that you bring from being in the temple?

You have quite steadily for quite some time thought along the same lines, watching for improvement, every day traveling the road of life. I'm seeing the hardship and the easy going, but if you have to turn around and hunt for a road and if it isn't as pleasant when you enter it, many times you take a detour right then. And there is then a lapse of time when you seem to do nothing. But the transition from one state of consciousness to a higher one is accomplished as we respond to clearer vision and absorb deeper truths. The auric channel becomes wider, the path more familiar, bringing health, happiness, and a sense of peace and power.

ANDREW All these beautiful, positive energies and colors ... they're part of awakening, they're integral to the Eightfold Path ... and awakening is key to overcoming.

JOHN BASINSKI For us on the Eightfold Path, awakening involves identifying our lions and being cleared of them. They're impediments, so we need to conquer them.

MARY We all had that experience as an awakening to life there. We're given the experience so that in going over after we pass, we have some concept that we're going to live over there just as we do here. The goal in awakening is to dissolve delusion to effect transformation. Enlightenment enables us to see reality as it is, opening ourselves to the indwelling spirit.

SYLVIA Mary, you spoke about the cup of nectar. I wanted to say that many of us had that experience in the temple this past week. This is what I brought back from that beautiful ceremony: At the beginning, I was in a room with a guide. My hands were bound with silken ropes in front, and I didn't know how to get rid of them or to even loosen them a bit. They didn't really hurt but they restricted me and I longed to be free of them.

I tried many times but just couldn't make any progress. Then suddenly, a shower of gold and silver rain descended all around me. There was no sense of water, only particles, beautiful tiny particles that bathed me and keep pouring down from above. Talk about manna from heaven! Now, as if blessed with the shower of these gold and silver particles, my hands were easily freed by a miraculous power I didn't understand but welcomed in gratitude.

Right after that, I went to the ceremony where I was offered the cup of nectar. What a divine, incredible taste, like nothing I have ever experienced on Earth. I turned to see our entire class was present. Several of us embraced each other. Each one of you accepted the cup. Everyone (at least everyone I saw) had passed the tests we were given. For me, loosening the bonds was the main part of it, I think.

******

REVIEW VIII
THE AURA, KEYNOTE AND KEYNOTE COLOR

Etheric substance is that which is seen by many as the first level above the level of the material, an emanation surrounding and extending beyond the physical body. This is called the aura. The aura is the area in which we sense. Under scientific scrutiny the aura is often called the energy field, which scientists have described as light radiating from the body in the form of photons. Pulsing, spiraling color energy emanates from man's divine center in the body, flows and extends outward in the form of photons moving at up to 200,000 cycles per second, forming the aura.

This aura or energy field is a primary communicator between living species. We affect one another through our auras — we're aware of `chemistry.' When two auras are harmonious, the chemistry is there; inharmonious auras lead to discord. The aura can be large and bright in the healthy person, and greatly diminished in a person who is unhealthy. The major part of our auras are ever changing with the shifting circumstances and vicissitudes of life. When we lose control, such as in an anger flare up, the spiritual aura goes.

Clairvoyants have seen auras extending to a great distance. In Mary's color classes, we studied the seventeen Permanent Rays of a Master and their qualities, qualities we looked to develop in ourselves.

On the spiritual level, the human aura is defined as the Kingdom of the Soul, and the Color path is a mystical journey toward the soul's development. Color opens the door to self unfoldment. It is the way of mental illumination and intuitive perception. The wise man makes the world his initiation chamber, life itself the threshold of the mysteries. Those who would make true progress should look on everything that happens to them in life as an initiation trial, and so become their own initiators.

The 7th Ray of the Spiritual Arc of Yellow is the ray one looks for first when reading an aura, this ray being the source of illumination and supply to the aura. The striped colors of this ray are, right to left: yellow-orange; deep rose; pastel rose tinted with white light; and pale yellow. The orb within this ray can be either very pale yellow or rich sun yellow, according to the person's spiritual development. Its location also indicates the degree of development the person has attained. Adding yellow to the rose creates the color of salmon pink, enlightens and lifts upward into spiritual life.

Every person possesses their own keynote of musical sound to which they vibrate. Each has a keynote of color which becomes their personal stimulation. Each projects his own aura of color vibrations emanating from within, flowing outward with many colors following the contour of the body after the manner of a cocoon or egg. The keynote color is above the head, the topmost color in the aura, that which holds the keynote sound enwrapped. As we develop, the spiritual aura widens and grows out.

Your keynote was given you when you came in to this world. It's a baby's first cry. What does your keynote do? It vibrates through the entire being and becomes a chord of color music in your life. Getting in touch with your keynote and keynote color are important tools in spiritual development.

SEVENTH STEEP   To the TEMPLE OF THE FOURTH DIMENSION

First Station: OPENNESS. Openness is being fluidic in all three bodies to the inflow of spiritual revelation.

Second Station: ACCEPTANCE. Acceptance requires a willingness to set ones own choices aside where or when they are contrary to spiritual direction.

Third Station: ADJUSTMENT. Adjustment requires flexible response in all three Bodies to fulfill or act upon the spiritual guidance.

Fourth Station: ASSURANCE. Assurance is the declaration in full confidence of spiritual guidance received through the alignment of the three bodies.

Fifth Station: DIVINE IMAGINATION. This is the mirrored reflection of symbolic truth, a code to be deciphered by the seeker.

Sixth Station: COMPREHENSION. Comprehension requires the capacity of mind to fully understand through the apperception of the alignment of the three bodies. (Apperception: Inner perception, that which is first.)

*****

TEMPLE OF THE FOURTH DIMENSION

On the Steep of the Fourth Dimension, we go through the Stations of Comprehension, Imagination, Assurance, Adjustment, Acceptance, Openness, Absorption.

MIRIAM WILLIS The Stations on this Steep test us and reveal six main qualities of being that require growth and lifting in fourth dimensional reality. Not only does the necessity for testings penetrate our consciousness, but also the privilege of such opportunities fills one's soul with awe and reverence.

MARY The Fourth Dimensional Temple is called "the clearinghouse of man's emotional body." Our meeting place in the Temple of the Fourth Dimension was a vast space containing numerous assembly rooms. The room where we congregated, immense in its unbelievable expanse and majesty, was like nothing I had ever beheld. I have no words to describe it. There was music – music that vibrated to the song that had been developing in my soul, only more glorious, more triumphant, more divine. It was a vibration of power so alive it could be felt and seen. With colors in fluid harmony, it flowed out from the very bosom of eternity to exalt, redeem and bring to mankind the "peace that passeth all understanding." A faint echo still remains in my being.

HELEN MARSH I was looking down on a beautiful landscape with clusters of trees; there was this incredibly green lawn. I tried to reach out to see if I could see a temple. I didn't. That part blacked out and next I saw a beautiful violet colored light to the left, and a window with a large pane of frosted glass, actually more pebbled than frosted. A beautiful golden light was shining through that window. That blacked out, and I saw a dark figure in a white robe. He seemed to be talking. I next saw a group in a semi-circle; I was among them. They were in the dark, but light shone on their faces. I believe we were all standing there listening to a teacher.

MARY That's in the Temple of the Fourth Dimension, seeing through. Yes. Very fine.

From his experiences in the 9th Plane Temple of the Fourth Dimension, the neophyte journeys along the upward Steep, stopping to receive ever deepening knowledge of reality through his expanding capacity. He learns to see more clearly into the heart of his own being, penetrating to the root motives of his thoughts and actions. This awakens such desire for truth that he seeks to return many times to this temple to recharge his powers for further growth.

Without development in the human soul, we find ourselves loathe to believe in anything very great, because we turn continually back within ourselves for power, and we find ourselves seeing the faults in life, overlooking that which would lift us as well as the other person. That ego must become absent.

It's truly imagination that makes the difference between souls, not intellect or shrewdness. All the real things of life: sympathy, the power of entering into fine relations, loyalty, patience, devotion, goodness – seem to grow out of the power of imagination. The more you think of that, the more you realize its truth. We thought lightly of imagination, and we've often said, "Don't let your imagination run away with you," or get the better of you, but it takes a power of imagination to enter into the feelings of other people. It's associated with all the sensitivity of being, and this is why it's such a soul quality.

ANDREW Is there any sense of sectarianism in the Fourth Dimensional Temple? For instance, a Christian side, a Jewish side, and so forth?

MARY In our night work, Christian and Hindu, Jew, Muslim, Buddhist alike, all accept the temples because of the opportunity for growth that takes place in the divine progression of the soul. That fourth dimension is for every person who can square his life up with the spiritual. So we'll say it's a temple foursquare, with the possibilities of meeting every man's need. We all go to great temples along the way, and for specific training, you'll find each sect on its own is not contradicted. But in the merging in the 13th Plane, usually our temples come pretty close together, and we learn that it's one God, one greet Jehovah, one Master of all mankind. And man realizes when he's traveled that far that he's reached the plateau of confidence in God, and he stands clear of the fascinating thought that he's the only man that has it right.

ROWENA Do you mean that until we attain the 13th Plane, it's difficult for us not to believe we're the only ones that have it right?

MARY I believe the "rightness of opinion" stays with man, and we're subjected to the questioning ourselves. Say we find ourselves on the 13th Plane rather than the 9th. We'll find ourselves Jew and Gentile. The sects, the different feelings that they have, promoting the thing that appeals to most of them – in other words, somewhere behind us is our ego, trailing. And that's a rich thing to remember, because we have to leave it behind us sometime. And that's fine. Without an ego where would we be? But the ego should be subservient to the highest in man. If we have the will to believe in what has come to us as life's experience, and that experience can be accepted, balanced, and used, forging ahead with patience and understanding, we meet the needs of life for development of the human soul.

Man has a right to his own thoughts, but unless he changes those thoughts, his character won't change, for our ideals and the building of our thought life is what we are. And it shows forth in our character and our understanding of other people. There's nothing static in life. Life doesn't stand still. Conditions change. Conditions are changing every day of our lives. We must grow with them. Therefore, these old "set" modes and ideas will have to be left behind if we're to make progress.

ROWENA Well then, it's ego that makes them ...

MARY Let us define "Ego." The Ego – a person could be, to me, egoistic, want the best for themselves and everyone else, but "egotistic" goes a step further and says that "I'm right." You're right today and wrong tomorrow.

GLENN But some people can't see that. They think they're always right.

MIRIAM WILLIS I had a feeling all day long today, a conviction that I could bring something through. And the day was just one thing after another; there really wasn't an opportunity to sit down and do this writing that I felt I could do by lifting myself to a higher vibration. And so I said to the good Father, "Well, if you want me to write it, there'll be an opportunity for me to do it; if not, it doesn't matter."

I was standing at the sink cleaning pans, and thinking about this Temple of Fourth Dimensional Consciousness. And to me, it was not like a temple; it was a consciousness. And I seemed to enter it in a realization that one was permitted to go there to receive the reality of Fourth dimensional consciousness and the integration into one's being, and that this is really what happened to me in that temple, and that one was permitted to see the actual operation of the law in the reflected colors within the aura, and to see when certain rays had been brought to maturity, and that when they were brought to maturity, this was the fourth dimensional consciousness or state of being which then would never leave one.

MARY Forty years ago, I wrote the story of the Fourth Dimensional Temple. Today, because I didn't remember, I had to sit down and think it out, so I turned and went in reverse, backwards. When I finished writing, I showed Miriam something that seemed to her like she had read it before. We compared the two, and I brought back almost the same thing, practically word for word, from forty years ago. You see what I'm trying to tell you? What we gain we keep. We don't lose it.

SANDRA I know there's a color ray we often use for when someone might want to hog the show too much, in order for that person to realize they should step aside and allow another person to shine.

MARGARET That's the 11th ray of the Spiritual Arc of Red: "Tenderness and concern for a brother, stepping in the shade that others may shine. "

SANDRA Well, I think I've all too often had the exact opposite situation in my life, in being guilty of "hiding my light under a bushel," not giving credit where credit is due – to myself! Here's my temple lesson: in this experience, I was a close friend of the First Lady of the United States over a period of several years, beginning in childhood. I knew her so well, cared deeply about her, and had a great desire to write an official biography of her, for which I'd need her permission, but I didn't want to use our friendship for a favor, so I hesitated to bring the subject up to her. For my own edification, I wrote 50 pages about her, read them over and was surprised how good they were.

I knew I was the ideal person for this undertaking, and had finally convinced myself that it was all right to gingerly approach my lifetime friend the First Lady to ask her permission to allow me to write this book on her. Imagine my chagrin when I found that an unqualified, inexperienced young lady by the name of Linda, who had real chutzpah, had brazenly gone to the First Lady and signed her to a contract to permit her to have the rights to the First Lady's story. I had been aced out, I who really was the deserving one! It was a lesson to me to value myself more than I too often do, and I was shown that instead of being so ready to step aside, I need to assert myself and step forward.

VIOLET We're always given exactly what we need. I'm always amazed at that. The teachers over there know us far better than we know ourselves.

ESTHER BARNES In this Fourth Dimensional Temple, I had a vision of a tree that was perfectly round. It was in the color of the 9th ray of the Spiritual Arc of Blue, meaning "truth of self attained." The tree was made up of beautiful small triangles. They were so stylized, as if it were just all these triangles inside of a circle, and the base of it came down, and then it became a triangle at the base, and it was flashed to me twice, as if it was to be impressed on me very strongly. Then in meditation, I had a vision of sparkling triangles that filled a door. The center was blue plum, the color of depth of love, the 3rd Ray of the Spiritual Arc of Purple. I know that this ray encompasses and goes far beyond human love. Through this ray, one touches the fundamental motivation for being in this life. The silvery film, or "bloom," is the touch of the Christ spirit.

MARY That's very wonderful for you; yes indeed. I'm glad you got it, dear. I believe that your triangles, Esther – the triangle is in all symbolism, supposed to be something that extends from the Tree of Life, and the point of it is supposed to be the heaven world and God. Now Greek literature gives the Tree of Life in a triangle. And then in the Egyptian, in the temples you'll find – in fact, many of the old friezes that were around the temples, you'll find that the king's men were always carrying the Tree of Life, and it was a triangle.

DIANA DAVIS I also had an experience in the Fourth Dimensional Temple. I was standing in front of five or six containers containing liquids. I started emptying them, and scarcely thinking about what I was doing, quickly emptied all but one. Suddenly, I realized I must not pour out the final container, and in fact really should not have emptied the first ones, either. But now all I had was this one last precious container, and I must absolutely keep this one full at all costs. It was a moment of reckoning. It's like a realization where you recognize your mistakes, and understand that now you have but one chance left and you can't blow it. You have finally wised up and you're going to do it right this time, do or die. "I was blind but now I see ..." And I know I have to do something about it with my newfound understanding.

CONNIE SMITH It's amazing how symbols can be so personal, how they carry so much meaning and impress us so deeply.

VIOLET May I say right at this point: wouldn't that be the raising of your physical seeing into the higher seeing?

MIRIAM Well, it's, like a physical vibration that reaches the spiritual, and you mount on it, which is the same thing, I think.

MARY We answer when we enter the fourth dimensional vibration, and that's the proof of it.

MIRIAM ALBPLANALP You mentioned about the clearinghouse of man's emotional body being up there, and I guess I've been one of the best customers of that place. Are there different degrees of testing tools that they use, so that the air and water testings are emphasized? Because I had a very severe type of electric testing, so I hopefully thought surely they were getting some difficult things cleansed out of me.

MARY We'd have to take it out of the physical and put it into the mental. Then that has to be somehow radiated from the spirit in order to take away that one thing, that habit, or something that's been a pressure that held your progress. Then we go on our way, discovering, and they would probably send you back after that testing to the Temple of Remembrance and see if you could pick up the thing that has stayed there blocking your progress.

MIRIAM ALBPLANALP I couldn't figure out what it was, but I thought it was encouraging when I got that shock treatment.

MARY And you know we really need a shock treatment sometimes to get out of our minds that we can't recover from some fault. Do you realize that? Because many people suffer over a fault; they can't see that there's any way of recovering from it and so they walk along with it. It becomes a sickness after a while. We do need to exorcise if the mind becomes inured with ideas you can't get rid of. Exorcising is the thing that we really need, to change the circulation.

GEORGE Mary, do you have any tips how we should go about trying to remember our night work?

MARY When you wake in the morning after having slept, first of all, thank God for that rest, for that sleep. Then as you stand for a moment in the holy presence, see if you receive something, if something does come back, perhaps just something fleeting – any words or picture. You probably should write it down.

MARGARET I would also recommend meditation, best in the morning, at least for me. That's when I bring back many of my recollections. I climb the Channel, I rest in the fullness of the Fount of Supply, and my night work starts coming back.

EVA Automatic writing can work well, too.

MARY In Sanskrit, the Hindu says, "If God wished to hide, God would choose man to hide in, because that is the last place man would look for God." So we're seeking, searching everywhere outside ourselves for God, attending countless lectures, meetings, joining groups, looking for leaders, when all the time God is waiting within us. Through Color and meditations each of us becomes aware of the benefits of spirit. Because of the training you've received in these temples, you know the meaning of development of the fourth dimensional expression, because you're right in that very sound track of vibration that sets up every response to God's love in action.

How does one live in fourth dimensional consciousness? By breathing in through spiritual colors the universal wisdom that permeates all space. In a sense we become inspired by generating Color within ourselves, by disciplining our bodies to serve as channels to receive currents of universal mind to be transformed into creative energy.

MIRIAM WILLIS Isn't this the reason it's helpful to look at some material creation in color, and it becomes a step up to the spiritual. You know, I couldn't get it for the longest time. But now I realize that from the physical there is that vibratory tie, and it's like a springboard that you tie from, one step to the other.

JOHN BASINSKI At the lab where I work, everyone is engrossed in string theory, according to which there are at least ten dimensions in the universe. But I don't let this interfere with my acceptance of the term "fourth dimensional consciousness." They're separate subjects, separate concepts that are totally reconcilable.

FRANK And we always have to bear in mind that words we use to express the spiritual can be imprecise, inexact, and even contradictory.

VIOLET We just have to use another part of our intuitive perception, our imagination -- to understand.

*****

REVIEW IX
THE CHANNEL OF OUR BEING
THE KEYS TO THE KINGDOM

The Channel of our Being, or the Keys to the Kingdom, is one of Mary's greatest gifts to us. It is our spiritual connection between the earth plane and higher states of consciousness. The Channel is an inner spiritual spiraling pathway to Heaven beginning at the solar plexus and reaching through the crown of the head. This inner portion of a human being is the path of light leading one's consciousness to higher realms of understanding.

The Channel consists of twelve Keys to the Kingdom of the Soul, twelve spiritual colors being the inner portion of the human being that opens the way to illumination and intuitive perception. We access the Channel by climbing to an uplifted state, reaching the Fount of Supply. We also commune with it directly by visiting the Planes of Heaven in our sleep.

The Fount of Supply is the gateway between the visible and invisible worlds, an opening to fourth dimensional consciousness, a transcendence from the illusion of matter to "living in eternity now," where we become acutely aware of the oneness of our two worlds. Each Channel color gives uplift and support to the spiral above it, as we work our way up the colors, drawing them to ourselves for a few seconds at a time. Because each succeeding color is of a higher vibration than the one below it, you "climb" in consciousness while ascending the Channel. You may become aware that the Channel is like a vibrating stream of rapidly changing light as the Colors of the Channel begin to revolve with the movement of a kind of inner sleeve and to shed radiant light. Those are the stronger lights of the auric Channel.

Beginning with the color of royal purple at the bottom, proceed upward, and either audibly or silently name each color: "I stand in the royal purple of faith and mount to the gray lavender of the holding force of patience, the pink lavender of inspiration, the rose lavender of the spiritual voice and the blue orchid of prophecy, over the yellow bridge of enlightenment to the rose orchid of the message bearer, the red lilac of the holding force for the Band of Teachers, over the bridge of yellow enlightenment to the glowing peach of union of mind and spirit, the light blue orchid of brotherhood, the blush orchid of serenity, over the bridge of lightest green in desirelessness to the rose bisque of grace and the light blue lavender of peace. And now I stand at the Fount of Supply."

At the word "peace," rest in the quietude of your lifted spirit in silent expectancy. This is a time of communion with the Infinite, where a door to the world beyond opens. This is a time of communion with the Infinite. The union of our two worlds is realized by opening the Channel and seeing with the spiritual eye clearly into the higher planes. You have climbed the Channel, and when you return, you have a spiritual extra sense that you've brought with you.

Climbing the Channel is a good way to begin a meditation. We can refine and balance our chakras, our mind and emotions, our spiritual being, with daily use of the Channel. When one can sense the soothing rays of color, one knows he can accomplish the next rung on the Planes of Heaven. We can't create a miracle, but we can be a part of one by holding the force of power in color for that miracle to happen. While in the Channel, we bypass the lower astral realms and are never exposed to negative forces. We're protected.

****

> EIGHTH STEEP To the AREA OF RECREATION and the TEMPLE OF CHANNELED POWER
>
> First Station: ABSORPTION. Here the inflow of developing grace acts as a catalytic transformer to incorporate the three bodies in fluidic, assimilated balance.
>
> Second Station: DESIRE. Here one is trained to recognize his personal desires and to lift them through the alignment of his three bodies to the mesa of desirelessness, where they are confirmed or rejected.
>
> Third Station: INTELLIGENCE. Intelligence is the faculty to know the sum total of Infinite Intelligence that leads the seeker on the path of mystical perfection to develop the eternal quality of choice.
>
> Fourth Station: MOTIVATION Motivation is a propelling force within, which leads to action.
>
> Fifth Station: ILLUMINATION. By the power of Infinite Intelligence the mind becomes supplied with light through which the soul reaches complete understanding in the spiritual order. Four A's that lead to illumination: aspiration, awareness, acceptance, adoration.
>
> Sixth Station: ACTION. Action is the higher octave of creative energy reflected by the soul that man may put into directed action the pattern of his life.

Our tests on the Stations of the 8th Steep include absorption, desire, intelligence, illumination, motivation and action. One begins to realize that in the heavenworld there is a great continuity of purpose and sequence of enabling grace, where the soul seeks to replenish his centers of God power.

******

AREA OF RECREATION

MARY We travel again and again to the Area of Recreation. The emphasis on gratitude, reiterated each night during the past week, opened our consciousness to the inflow of receptive force, and one found building power in the Area of Recreation, where the whole of our lives blossomed with renewed energy, lifting the soul's desire toward ever greater fulfillment. This impetus provided courage to follow the "beam," and one found his powers newly born in the Area of Recreation.

VIOLET In this temple, I was told to "question not, but write down what's given you." So this is what I received, after meditating on my nighttime experience in the Area of Recreation: "Forces touching elements. Rivers of power. Focused energy. Flow of such might, affinities recognized and utilized. All this can be incorporated in the life, even if not understood. Laws can be recognized. Don't be afraid of them as they play about you. They're demonstrable. You exist in the midst of them, even if the human mind can't grasp the immensity of such forces."

MIRIAM WILLIS This is where we were last night, in the 9th Plane Area of Recreation. There are tremendous resources at the Fount of Supply. One of the lessons we learn here is how connections are made so the power can be utilized.

BARBARA I saw an intense, deep rose light. A teacher who spoke with us said, "Make your group the most precious contacts of your life, a privilege and blessing. It's sacred, because it was sealed with the light and love of the Masters. Drink in all you can possibly hold, but give to each other in like measure. Climb forever upward, keeping eyes ahead and vision high. Remember, brotherhood means love and giving. Creation is a continuous process requiring our help. Help the onward evolution. Your contribution is an essential part of the whole. Even the lowly earthworm is needed in the economy of God."

DIANA In my night work in the Temple of Recreation, I saw various symbolic images in different sizes. I kept trying to make various objects, all possessions I own, fit into small size containers, but it was a tight fit and they would not compress enough to make it. Then I suddenly realized that it was not my possessions, but I myself that I was trying to fit into these too small containers. I saw that there was a larger container I would be able to fit into that would provide plenty of room to contain me, but I hesitated to go there, because I was afraid.

By my side was a guide who did not insist, but was very gently reassuring me to acknowledge the larger picture. After considerable resistance, I finally accepted heavenly guidance, stopped fighting, acquiesced and allowed myself to enter the larger container. The fit was perfect. I immediately felt a sense of rightness that I belonged here. Why had it taken so long for me to realize this?

In my waking self, I understood the meaning of this test, which I'm sure was a test of fear – it meant change, adapting, overcoming stubborn resistance, to finally acknowledge the inevitability of change, understanding that to keep fighting, resisting and denying was contrary to my own best interests. Upon waking, I had a flash of insight that this lesson or test – or both lesson and test – meant something new and positive had been built into my consciousness. It was as if a deeper part of me had received very important training, almost like an answer to an unuttered prayer had been granted with this scenario on the Other Side, and my character had been molded much for the better.

******

TEMPLE OF CHANNELED POWER

MIRIAM WILLIS We were delighted to be granted the privilege of visiting the Area of Recreation many times, grateful for the power recreated there that enabled us to climb ever higher toward unfoldment. In this refreshment we were lifted toward the Temple of Channeled Power, which is located on the left side of the chart.

MARY With the fragrant air becoming ever more rarified and with a vibrant lifting quality of concentrated strength, we seem not to touch the ground as we advance. Beneath our gliding motion we see great beauty of flowers, bluest waterways, verdure, trees of rare lace character caressed by gold and silver light surrounding the Temple of Channeled Power. We are aware of many high slender spiraled towers of exquisite beauty that look like translucent alabaster that sparkle in scintillating glory.

Each seeker is drawn to the entrance he is attracted to, and enters a doorway of palest green. Within, he stands alone on a slab of the same color. This contact imparts a power of centralizing one's forces and opening his consciousness in one pointed direction, upon which power he ascends the spiral of his own channeled forces. Having left his thinking body, in this freed suspension, he is conscious only of quickening power and elevation.

At the height of this experience, he is aware of entering a vast area in which every channeled tower becomes part of one great galleria around a well-like opening of an exquisite font of delicate beauty that exudes endless power, gentle yet sufficient for all needs. One's consciousness knows this is the Fount of Supply. Fragrance, music and song issue in perfect harmony and rhythm, echoing in cadences far above one's powers of extension.

This is followed by a great stillness and expectancy of reverent awe, as a glorious canopy spreads above us, and the voice of our beloved Master Jesus speaks: "In your surrender to channeled power, all heaven is revealed, truth and wisdom given. Be faithful."

ROWENA I climbed the Channel and reached the Fount of Supply. What awaited me were mostly rose and blue tones. There was a huge fountain. A Gothic cathedral appeared, tall but not wide, with a very narrow steeple. A bare headed priest, dressed in a white ceremonial robe, carrying a crook, appeared at a door. He said I was not ready to enter the temple. At the top of the Channel I was told I had come to the Temple of Channeled Power.

MARY Well, from there you would take your vibratory rating, and you would be activated if you were ready to go through the door. So probably the next time you'll make an entrance. We usually make three trips and are tested before we go in. Usually it's set opinions or prejudice that keeps us from that. If we search ourselves for our opinion of some person we've held a long time, and we can't admit that opinion is wrong, and if you describe why you had it, you may see you haven't any right to that opinion. So that's one of the reasons we often have to change our mind in order to enter temples. We're doing ourselves no good by putting a barrier between ourselves and development. When it comes to the human soul, you must have respect for the soul within that other person. And our likes and dislikes can interfere in our capacity for loving.

So it's easy for us to cheat sometimes, to take away any desire to love this one or to root for that one. But it's such a pleasure to do for those we love and take no credit. That's what always bothered me. The credit we seem to receive is what we do for those we don't love, who need our love. In other words we're correcting something within ourselves when we love someone who doesn't deserve it.

KATHY I would have to say that in my own case it would be a modified love, because I couldn't go all out and love certain persons unconditionally, although I could look at someone else and find it in my heart to. Selective love is what I'd have to say.

EVA It's been said that to love your brother who scorns you is the acid test.

MARY Now we do get to the place where you recognize they're all God's creatures, and then somehow you find yourself drawn to the soul of a particular human being. And you see the reality of what's wrong; many times, you're led to openly see. Sometimes, you must lift the mask and see that you've learned from that person. Haven't you learned, many times from people that within your heart you could scarcely tolerate? Because you've looked for the eyes of the Christ in their eyes just once, knowing that they need your soul understanding from what you really are. So development brings its crosses. Reading auras brings a cross. Then you have to look at that cross and say, every human being bears their cross. How do I know what I see that's wrong in you is not your cross?

JOHN BASKINSI These must be things we experienced in the Temple of Channeled Power, because what you're saying ties in perfectly with my own experience there.

MARY Instructions were given to our class in the Temple of Channeled Power. The great sun rising over the darkness of night – the great sun of righteousness being over the darkness of materialism

— these are God's answers; they're the law of his rhythm. When you stray, you break the rhythm of your life. Grasp this great truth. The broken chord must be brought back into the true tone again, and that process causes pain. When all is shepherded back into line and tune, God's answer comes with the rising sun. Greatness is born through the touching of heaven and earth. Life is an uninterrupted river. It sometimes flows out of sight, but it's there, and it can be contacted no matter where in the universe it may be flowing.

MARGARET I received a message when I woke. "All currents yesterday were serene. We could so easily come to you in your gathering. Our nearness was greater than our words. You all felt it. Power will manifest in different ways and degrees in each of you. Each and all must face the challenge of this life of masterhood in all its significance. Drop from your consciousness the words "time" and "age." They're not for the spirit of man, only for his temporal body and its temporary environment. The living soul of man, the real you, is above that: don't hinder it by the dominance of devised things or ideas. Freedom must be like the breeze from heaven. Breathe in the breath of God and realize its significance. Live this and give this."

EVELYN What Margaret said seems applicable to me. Also applicable is my experience in the ordering of personal power, how we often resist our own spiritual power, yet inevitably we do acknowledge it, embrace it and are stronger for having recognized it. It's like recognizing the God within.

GRACE It's such a blessing to experience Heaven every night as we do – such fullness, that world as we know it.

MARY The Other Side is a place of hope, compassion, justice, opportunity, benevolence and tranquility. It's walking in still waters. We feel the evidence of a guiding hand. It's a perfected place where truth shines through; the soul, set free, hears the call to the beyond, knowing that higher initiations await revelation into the plan of the ages. The Other Side is a world of organization and beauty. It holds out to every living human being his own Plan of Life, a plan of harmony and happiness, if they have so accepted.

We realize that life on the other side is very much like this our present life, except with a greater degree of refinement. We find landscapes similar to those on Earth, including every type of tree and flower, mountains, bodies of water, but everything is far, far more beautiful and ordered. One becomes aware of many shrines for rest, meditation and devotion to cultivation of the inner life.

One enters these heavenly sanctuaries of spiritual power for renewal and refreshment. When we're in our night work, we walk on grass, we see the lakes and rivers, flora and fauna. And when we pick the fruit or the flower, they appear again in all their beauty and fullness, as though we hadn't touched them. Truth is all about us, and it's withheld from no one.

The heavenly paths are very beautiful if you once get the inner you to really achieve the concept of that Path. Over there, faith can absolutely, literally move mountains. Over there, nothing is impossible and everything is possible. If we can just capture a fraction of that for our Earth lives ... imagine what we could do.

MIRIAM WILLIS Sometimes it really feels like magic over there, when you see those heavenly mountains being moved, and it's you that's doing the moving. But you see that really, it isn't magic at all – it's our own power that's able to do these things. We're impelled by Jesus' words: "These things I do, shall ye do also, and greater."

EMILY Christ is said to be a 2000th Plane soul. This means there are many, many planes beyond the ones we study here, and that we could some day make it to there. At least, Jesus says we could.

MARY And you know, this great one is yours; this great one is mine. I often think, meditating on the blessedness of all that which we have, if we will but use it. A river of light is flowing in the world today. Not all recognize it or know its source, but its power is at work. Pray for this power to multiply exceedingly so that illumination may come, and peace come out of the fires of men – peace in the heart, peace in the nations and peace as the real foundation of world brotherhood. The avenues to God are truly many. Pray for them and have tolerance. Souls are on different levels, where one or another "avenue" is the only one they can take. Be deeply thankful for all your blessings. Pass these two powers along – love and gratitude.

*****

REVIEW X
THE EIGHTFOLD PATH

When Guatama Buddha rediscovered the Eightfold Path, it was already a very ancient and remarkable teaching, universal in application and ageless in wisdom, known to have existed as early as ten thousand years previously. Its principles were taught in ancient Persia, Egypt, India, Tibet, China, Palestine, Syria, and Greece. Scriptures describe an ancient path that was practiced by all previous Buddhas.

The Eightfold Path is contained in the fundamental concepts of Brahmanism, the Vedas, the Upanishads and the Yoga systems of India. In Palestine and Syria, members of the brotherhood followed the Eightfold Path. The teaching appears in the Zend Avesta of Zoroaster, who translated it into a way of life followed for thousands of years. The Essenes were devout followers of the Eightfold Path. Jesus, a member of the Essenes, taught the same principles. Buddha's sacred Bodhi tree is correlated with the Essene and Egyptian Tree of Life. In Tibet the teaching found expression in the Tibetan Wheel of Life.

The Eightfold Path teaching explains the Law, showing how man's deviations from it are the cause of his troubles, and gives us the method out of our dilemma. By altering distorted views and replacing them, suffering is eased; as one works toward eradicating negative dispositional traits such as greed, hatred, and delusion, one develops insight into the true nature of reality.

The Noble Eightfold Path is the fourth of the Four Noble Truths of the Buddha's teachings regarding suffering and its extinction leading to liberation. The Four Noble Truths are: the Noble Truth of Suffering, the Noble Truth of the Origin of Suffering, the Noble Truth of the Extinction of Suffering, and the Noble Truth of the

Path that leads to the Extinction of Suffering.

Buddha's Noble Truths explain the reality that life is suffering, pain, anguish and affliction, the cause being grasping, clinging to desire and aversion, and ignorance of the three marks of existence: that all things are unsatisfactory, impermanent, and without essential self. Existence is painful because of the illusion of our own identity, because of our ego focusing on itself as if it were separate.

The Eightfold Path gives us a way to the cessation of suffering, achievement of self-awakening, insight into the true nature of phenomena and a way to eradicate delusion. We see on this Path that everything in life is in a state of flux; that everything that arises will cease; and that our very existence is based on impermanence.

The Eightfold Path offers a solution leading toward self awakening and liberation. Practicing the Path awakens within the heart an intuitive knowledge that can solve both personal issues and problems of the world. We find on the Path that recognition is the first step in awareness. This is awakening. Next comes intent, with a change in heart and mind, leading to the conquest of one's emotional nature, to liberation from the past, and ultimately to Nirvana.

Perfecting the self is a process during many lifetimes that ultimately results in the state of freedom from suffering and rebirth. This is the Eightfold Path. In embracing the Eightfold Path, we're working to break old molds so as to obliterate our "lions." In this, we're greatly helped on the Other Side, and by Color.

*****

> NINTH STEEP   To the TEMPLE OF VIBRANT CONSCIOUSNESS
>
> First Station: RELEASED. Letting go of all that hinders soul development. Free of old ways. Released from the bondage of the little self and old habits.
>
> Second Station: FREED. Here one learns to operate in the divine rhythm, which sets one free without waste of power. Liberated from earthly constraints. A clearing of consciousness.
>
> Third Station: VITALIZED. Regenerated. Life giving force renews vitality. One becomes more and more vitalized, identified with the Christ principle; therefore wiser in action strengthened in power, renewed in energy.
>
> Fourth Station: SHEPHERDED. Through magnetic kinship one listens and obeys in guided protection.
>
> Fifth Station: EASED. Power within causes one to operate in balance. Centered in his awakened consciousness, the seeker becomes steadfast in this polarization.
>
> Sixth Station: AWAKENED. As one responds to this light within. its radiance awakens all faculties to living reality.

*****

TEMPLE OF VIBRANT CONSCIOUSNESS

MIRIAM WILLIS   We go up the Steep to the Temple of Vibrant Consciousness. It seems that every potential power blossoms in the exquisite richness of its own color, and that all qualities reach the apex of their maturity in this temple, to the zenith of 9th Plane consciousness.

As one approaches this temple, his own potential qualities in vibrant color rays extend to him. He enters a golden door arrayed in these colors. He is breathless, charged with greater power into which he nestles. His whole being responds to this embrace. He not only feels secure, but he realizes the truth of the saying, "Let go and let God," for he is doing nothing but responding, yielding utterly to sustaining force. Never again will he struggle to develop; rather he will rest in the power in complete faith and loving gratitude. He is aware of a great throng of angelic hosts, and is filled with the beauty and harmony of their exquisite music.

VIOLET' As we approached the Temple of Vibrant Consciousness, there issued from the temple a soft, delicate sassing sound. It felt like the music of the spheres. One was aware the sound was not confined to this temple alone, but came from a vast space – a beautiful rhythmic hum that included the whole universe of created worlds.

The temple stood in a soft, blueish light, incandescent and indescribable in quality. Entering, we walked toward an altar. Crystal columns and pendants all reflecting and refracting into millions of flashing points of light greeted me. It was so utterly sublime that I was drawn into a state of near ecstasy from the beauty and marvel of it all. Above and beyond what one understood through sight and sound was the consciousness of an element of sweet, gracious protection, the awareness of a sense of motherhood, feeling the feminine side of God's nature, which was to my consciousness pleasant and lovely. It was something of much greater vastness, a penetration as though one had been let into a rare, sublime consciousness just for oneself.

One had been allowed to perceive something that was being given to them alone, as a precious gift out of the eternal storehouse of God's wonders. We absorbed the beauty and grasped what "vibrant consciousness" truly is It's a deep well within one's being where the wonder of God's greatness and power dwells.

MARY In this Great Temple of Vibrant Consciousness, life's symphony flows through the magic tones of harmony and rhythm. Spirit is the universal life taking shape and flowing through all forms.

When we entered the temple, the angelic hosts were gathered, and the air was vibrant with melody. Music is the unfathomable speech leading to the infinite, the fulfillment of all expression. It's the singing of the spheres made alive in painting and in sculpture, voiced in drama and symphony. Whatever the setting, the fire of creation vibrates throughout all manifested forms.

I asked the great teacher to speak of friendship. He answered, "Real friendship unmasks the soul. It's not a cloak to put on and take off, but is the divine radiance of God ever turned outward, a holy trust born of understanding. Cherish it."

I asked of wisdom. "Wisdom is spiritual vision and comes through intuition. It takes no account of vagaries of the mind. Learning is an ever widening process; though a man be filled with learning, learning is but a path to wisdom." His wise words were balm to my spirit.

The vapors that cover Earth in early dawn brim with life, and when the evening air is filled with mist, Earth breathes forth fragrance. Sorrows in life are like that. Often when troubles beset us, sweet scented qualities come forth – patience, charity, tenderness. The shade of the passing sunset fades our yesterdays, and the dawn of sunrise brings a new day.

Creative power through Color is unfoldment. It's a rearranging of material given man to wear within the weaving of his life's pattern, as songs or poems are all in a state of development.

Outward expression is an expansion of consciousness. When we're in tune with life's harmony, we become conscious of growth in creation taking place. So lift your chalice to be filled; the cup is withheld from no man in tune with life's harmony. Faith brings understanding. Bless you, all of you dear ones.

HELEN MARSH In a temple experience Tuesday night: I found myself slowly floating along an avenue lined with dense shrubbery. Evenly spaced behind the shrubs were trees in full leaf. As I moved along, engulfed in and appreciating the serenity and its color of blush orchid, a beautiful talisman was placed in front of my hand. Then I was standing in a temple looking up towards the ceiling high above me, beautifully frescoed in soft rose and blue in a very elaborate design.

MARY That's our temple of this week, the Temple of Vibrant Consciousness.

ESTHER BARNES   In meditation, I had a vision of myriads of long, diamond shaped petals; all of the flowers I saw were made of these petals in that shape.

MARY   When we go into the Temple of Vibrant Consciousness, we see that the whole frontal piece extends way up in a peak and comes down ... that's what it is.

VIOLET   Does it have lilies on it?

MARY   No, the floor has lilies in it, not that frontal piece.

LOLA   Mary, on the trip I recently took, the autumn coloring was so wonderful, and I had an experience that caused me to wonder if it's possible during the day to have a re-creation of the Temple of Vibrant Consciousness. I'd been looking at this glorious fall coloring in all the trees. I was thanking God for all the beauty, when suddenly it was just as if I had pulled a blind down; I began getting a flash with pictures. It was like the scene had been raised into a higher vibration, and it was so luminous. It was just the most wonderful experience!

MARY   That is illumination, one point of illumination. It usually comes that way.

MARGARET   I too had glimpses and impressions of beautiful autumn colors. One scene in which these colors were prominent seemed to have a series of madonna-like figures lifting up babies. Would there be a special Thanksgiving service over there in which they gave thanks for these youngsters?

MARY   Could easily be. Well, I'll tell you, it's a Hindu rite, if nothing else. The last-born is always taken at this time of year, harvest time. Usually our Thanksgiving coincides with the Hindu rite, which is usually the last part of November, when babies are brought to the temple and blessed.

JEANNE   I recalled a water test: I was immersed in a body of water with a heavenly guide at my side. Also in the water with us was a small fish. His mouth had been injured and there was a gaping hole where the mouth should have connected to the rest of his head. I felt very sorry for this fish, who seemed almost human; I felt like he had a soul, a heart and mind. The guide told me the fish possessed a thin thread with which he could mend himself to fix the hole in his mouth.

All of a sudden that small, nearly invisible thread appeared. The fish tried to catch the thread but it slipped away. I tried to help the fish and I think on the third try the fish did catch the line. I felt relieved and encouraged that the fish would be able to heal himself, sew up that tear and be whole again. It was a very inspiring, positive experience, symbolic and very spiritual. Since this involved a fish, I think it may have had something to do with Chrisitianity and the Piscean Age.

LINDA CLARK How are we dressed on the Other Side? What do we wear? Are we in the same attire we're wearing in bed? Pajamas and nightgowns?

MARY You're in your spiritual body and you're wearing a loose, filmy robe that's quite dense. You pick it up and it's weightless, but you put it on, and you feel the weight of it. So we do feel weight; we do have sensations and pleasure.

SYLVIA Don't we get any new clothes over there? I thought we did.

MARY With that matchless material that's handed to us ... it's a web of something or other. Hold your hands up and you can clothe yourself in the most remarkable colors. If you're in rapport with the work and in harmony with the temple, if you want a robe of rose, you put rose on; if you want purple, you put purple around you. You frequently want to change clothes over there.

LINDA How do we do that?

MARY Stand still for about 20 seconds, think the new color, the new style, and you will have it. You can create your own wardrobe and wear it. The moment we start to come back, you'd love to bring it back with you.

*****

REVIEW XI
THE EIGHT PRACTICES
OF THE EIGHTFOLD PATH

All eight practices of the Eightfold Path begin with the word "right": right view, right intention, right speech, right action, right livelihood, right effort, right mindfulness, right concentration.

1. Right view, right belief or right understanding: an accurate vision of the nature of reality and the path of transformation. Right aspirations that lead to right attitudes toward others' beliefs, leading to wisdom.

2. Right intention, right thought, or right attitude: acting from love and compassion. An informed heart and mind.

3. Right action: an ethical foundation for life based on the principle of non-exploitation of self and others. Right conduct in every area; behaving in sincerity, simplicity and grace. Thoughtful consideration of others at all times.

4. Right speech: to speak only in kindness and love, with words of encouragement and helpfulness. Clear, truthful, uplifting and non-harmful communication.

5. Right livelihood: earning a living based on correct action and the ethical principal of non-exploitation. Choose a right mode of earning that is honest, in thrifty ways, that each shall carry his own responsibility.

6. Right effort: consciously directing our life energy to the transformative path of creative and healing action that fosters wholeness. Conscious evolution; moderate in all things; respect for self and all men. Fair in all transactions.

7. Right mindedness: anticipating the needs of others; discrimination

between our needs and our wants; to seek control of one's thoughts, developing awareness and mindfulness of oneself, one's feelings and thoughts, other people and reality. To seek mental maturity: the control of our thoughts.

8. Right concentration, or right meditation: entering reality through meditation; to plumb the depths and soar the heights, to find balance in life. Absorption or one-pointedness, not just of the mind, but also of the whole being in various levels and modes of consciousness and awareness. Enlightenment. To enter into reality through meditation. Mindfulness.

And with enlightenment comes liberation, Nirvana. It's been said that the only miracle Buddhism accepts is a change of heart; otherwise we would never be liberated from the past. We know that repeated action can change the nervous system physically, altering both synaptic strength and connections.

******

> TENTH STEEP To the AREA and TEMPLE OF DEVOTION
>
> First Station CALMNESS. Here one rests momentarily to give gratitude to God. Grace and trust are ingredients of calmness.
>
> Second Station QUIETNESS is a stillness of the mind and body in order that the still small voice may be heard. One learns here how to harmonize his will with the will of God.
>
> Third Station PURPOSE. Here one reviews the purpose of the current life and learns to unfold the purpose in daily living. The purpose of life is to know self/Self and follow one's true destiny path.
>
> Fourth Station QUALITY. Here one learns to compare the quality of one's living with the Christ standard.
>
> Fifth Station BREADTH. Expansion of consciousness. A maturing of spiritual life.
>
> Sixth Station DEPTH. Refinement of the life lived in faith and love.

*****

AREA and TEMPLE OF DEVOTION

MIRIAM The experience gained in the Temple of Vibrant Consciousness enables us to enter the Area of and Temple of Devotion.

MARY At the entrance to the Temple of Devotion, a vision was given us, and we saw the faces of the shining ones. They were serene as the light in which they shone, faces from which had faded all of Earth's desires. Even as we thrilled with the glory of the vision, we heard a voice. Faintly, and from down those far, shining heights, the voice rolled, chanting: "They needed not the lights of the sun, neither of the moon, for the glory of God did lighten them."

The vision passed. A white veil had fallen between us and all else. Then before us, like some splendid jewel, blazed a star of such magnitude and brilliance that even the snowy veil against which it hung seemed dim and dull by contrast. The beauty of the wondrous star, that ruby-hearted, golden-rimmed star – what could this mean? Then again came the voice of the Master, asking, "Does your soul not read the message?"

We saw whirling threads of red and yellow flame— conscious light and spirit. The truth streamed in upon each soul, for framed in the splendor of the vision was a form shadowy and divine which was slowly drawing us to the glory of its face. The star shone steadily into our eyes, and our garments were touched with its mellow light. We bowed in silence. We knew the heavenly movement of love was pouring forth, that singing is the harmonious breath of the Holy Spirit. We saw the youth of our times and their aspiration toward a world of peace and brotherhood. We saw the throng of people in all walks of life devoted to this fulfillment. The words came to one's conscious mind: "His name shall be called Counselor, the Mighty God, the Everlasting Father, the Prince of Peace."

In this temple, one becomes aware of many beautiful shrines for rest, meditation and cultivation of the inner life, and enters these sanctuaries of spiritual power for renewal and refreshment. Here also are many rhythmic laws built into one's being, enabling one to live more joyously and function at the 9th Plane level of consciousness.

VIOLET One sees many aspects of the Mother-Father principle of life in this Temple of Devotion, with the young nurtured by the devoted care of men and women. Everything here is perfection in natural beauty. Children's voices and laughter ring with joy like many silver bells. Mothers and fathers are ready to minister to every need, a strong, reliable bulwark. There are gardeners cultivating, pruning, gathering the fruit of their labors. A variety of occupations that need devoted care for their fulfillment fill the vast area. Each person performs his duty with love. In the completeness of experience that seems so natural in the heavenly spheres, one sees every stage of persevering effort and its fulfillment with a deep realization that devotion is responsible for its accomplishment.

A realization of the leveling out of things is impressed upon the soul, with an emphasis on the now of any situation—the laying aside of complaints, replaced by devotion to the task performed. The glory of devotion, so graphically displayed in this Area and Temple, reveals the joy of devoted service, and one realizes values not previously discerned.

MIRIAM WILLIS As we proceeded to the center of this Area, we beheld a most beautiful shrine over which many angels hovered. Here was enacted the preparation for the coming of Jesus. We were permitted to see, in panoramic view, Mary and Joseph – especially their devotion, their dedication and love for God and man. As we watched, it seemed natural and inevitable that they would be chosen by angel messengers to be the devoted guardians of the birth and nurturing of Jesus. We saw the call of the Wise Men from different parts of the world, brought together by the one purpose of pure devotion, which brings recognition of heavenly reality in earthly places. We saw the devotion of the shepherds to their duty – the expectation and hope in their hearts, and that beneath their crude garments, these were not ordinary men.

Then the scene changed, and we saw the real Christmas—the birth divine in modern times, the outer so utterly different, the inner just the same in the hearts of men, women and children. Overhead, the angels sang, and a great light rose from them to the throng below that merged with the glory of the heavenly beings.

MARY We're coming into that season when we must set up the crèche in our hearts and put the cradle clothes in, fresh and sweet, to adorn this beloved Christ. At this coming Christmastide we're reminded of a great preparation all over the world, and diligence in the preparation. This outward expression is a garment of generosity, an exchange of friendship and love that issues from a depth of something that is much greater than we are ourselves, that we're entering into.

Because we have glimpsed spiritual reality, we see and we know that the inner preparation is much greater and more important than the outer. Then sometimes, being as human as we are, we forget all this in the rush, hustle and bustle in the wondering of what we shall give to so and so and how can we afford this or that.

What we're trying to learn, to feel, to understand, to rise to in our consciousness, is the realization of the flowing power of that inner divine Christ touching and blessing everything with love, giving to us the discernment of what we should give and what we should hold. And this pattern has been the pattern throughout the ages, and its outward dress has been the ever changing garment and aspect of the inner.

MIRIAM WILLIS Let us think of ourselves identified with the Blessed Mother and with St. Joseph, as they expected the Lord Jesus, and prepare the inner citadel of our being to bear him in the arms of love, to cherish him and to nourish him. What an interwoven pattern of fulfillment that does present to us. And Color is like the swaddling clothes that keep the Christ child warm and comfortable, and helps us on our way to fulfill the reality of that divine presence.

MARY During this experience, one observes that at intervals everyone pauses to give thanks and praise in song, dance, thanksgiving and worship. The uplift and dignity of the commonplace created by devotion fills one with awe and an impetus to be devotedly faithful in all. Today, as then, the call is to stand steady and serene in the midst of turmoil and change, and to make straight the way for the coming light of the world.

AVIS I had a lovely vision in the Area of Devotion of a blue-painted archway of ellipse with stars. I was deeply aware of the devotion of our heavenly teachers, how they so lovingly guide us in our experiences in the invisible realms.

HELEN MARSH I'm trying to paint a vision. I was standing on a high rise of ground. Down below me was a large pond of incredibly clear water, and over to my right was an oblong building in a golden marble tone with a frieze around it. To my left was a semicircular building with columns around the outer edge—maybe six columns with wax around it that was partially in the picture. A green meadow surrounded this area.

MARY The southern court of the Temple of Devotion.

WOODIE I didn't bring anything back from the temple we visited, the Temple of Devotion, but I had a strong feeling that there was a special message in a lecture we attended there. Could you relay to us what was said by the teachers there?

MARY "Love is immortal. It buds on Earth and blossoms through eternity. Love opens up broad avenues through which Spirit may pass to higher and broader conceptions of life, and basks in the sunlight of truths of which the undeveloped mind knows nothing. Love quickens and inspires the mind. It exalts, softens, and glorifies the entire being. Its mystic charm transforms cold, commonplace life. It adorns Earth with the glory of Heaven, while its object takes on the highest attributes of the ideal. Love is a benediction, a baptism from the purest source of light. Love is a fragrance, a blending of all that is good. Love unlocks a door and opens a gate to the invisible world, the world of prayer and silence."

WOODIE Thank you, Mary.

MARY If you can get to the place where another is first, and go through life and love one human being better than yourself – it's one of the greatest tests that the world can give you, to feel I love one human being better than myself. And until a person does that, he can never go into complete development. Love is great; it incorporates all emotions. By love, you become enlightened; you become aware of God's power. We see it in others and we feel it in ourselves.

DAN When we have these tests in the temples, how are they chosen for us? Do the teachers over there decide what we need to undergo in testing?

MARY Your own soul determines your tests according to your plan of life and your spiritual awakening.

MARGARET I received this in the Temple of Devotion: "Stillness broadens the scope of the soul's evolution, widening its radius in the shining magnitude of love exhaled, as love's heavenly movement pours forth. Listen to the silent symphony breathing in waves of song, to the voice of God vibrating through the soul, creating music, mimicking divine glory."

MARY Let us keep this before us, that if there 's just one ray of harmony through every day, we're building stepping stones to greater reality. So let go, let life flow forth; give and receive.

PATTI I brought back this vision: a bird with a gold beak and feathers of many colors, chiefly yellow and rose. It flew toward my head and took something from my forehead. It had something to do with the third eye.

MARY Symbolic of the opening of the third eye.

RICHARD If I may venture to ask, is there a name for this beautiful, unusual teaching we're receiving from Mary in these classes and on the Planes at night? What is it called?

CARMEN (CHRISTINE) When people ask me that question, I've always called our teaching "esoteric Christianity."

ESTHER BARNES It combines the inner knowledge of many great wisdom schools – Judaism, Kabala, Buddhism, Hinduism, Theosophy, the Essene teachings – all that and a whole lot more.

DAN Because as we know, all sacred wisdom is derived from the same one great original ancient source. Different ages, different eras bring forth that knowledge to suit the times and the understanding of those who incarnate in that particular time.

ANDREW The most ancient, universal religion from which all later creeds and doctrines sprang once covered the entire known world.

MICHAEL The universe is the expression of a supreme conscious life, whether we call it God, Universal Mind, Jehovah, Allah, Brahma, the Almighty, or any other name.

DAN The Bible alone uses 72 different names for God.

ANDREW And every person has God within, a direct celestial ray from the One True Source, which we recognize as an inner presence – the imminent God.

MICHAEL And the other aspect of God, the transcendent God, is visible in his works, his creation, his universe.

VIOLET It's always seemed to me that in our spiritual bodies in our work on the Planes, as in our work on the Eightfold Path and hopefully also in our entire physical lives, we're expressing or endeavoring to express the two great commandments Jesus spoke of: loving God and loving our neighbor. All that is encompassed in the development we're working toward.

MARGARET "'Love the Lord thy God with all thy heart and with all thy soul and with all thy mind.' This is the first and greatest commandment, and the second is like unto it: 'Love thy neighbor as thyself.' On these two commandments hang all the Law and the Prophets."

GEORGE Our teaching is universal.

ESTHER BARNES It's such a gift. And too often, don't we take life for granted?

MARY I've often, said, oh God, open their eyes so that they might just once see, know it and feel the devotion of that world to us, and say "thank you!" I think of their devotion, so much so that we need never be fearful – there's always those everlasting arms, there's always that caring for us, waiting as a mother waits at the door for us to come.

VIOLET That's so true, Mary.

MARY In the name of the living Christ, we ask to be shown that which will help us to enact the life pattern that thou hast given us, oh Father;. Let us know where we've failed and let us enter with joy to every act of trust; and may our nights become as our days; and may our days be patterned as our nights, that our lives may be full and active in the work that we've been sent to do. For everyone who went through the tests in the temples, oh God, we thank thee, and we bow our heads in faith that we will be led on, night after night, through these same places of knowledge, until our wisdom becomes that which is golden and the threads of understanding binds them in love for those we walk with.

*****

REVIEW XII
"LIONS" ALONG THE WAY

Suppressed negative patterns stagnate development. Stumbling blocks on the path of development we call "lions on the path" or "lions along the way." Lions are undesirable dispositional qualities that we need to get rid of. They crop up again and again. They are your bad habits, your set opinions, guilty pleasures and secret little sins, the jealousies you don't even recognize, the vanities you excuse. Some lions hide from our awareness; some appear in unexpected ways. Some one might even consider to be virtues, but are actually traps in disguise. Sometimes we're even proud of our lions and wear them as a badge of honor. These hidden things in us need to be recognized, cleared up and swept out.

In dealing with the ego along the Eightfold Path, stress is laid on the mastery of pride and the control of likes and dislikes. We seek to confront these lions and subdue them. To change ourselves, we need to take charge of our mental attitudes and emotions. Self control over actions, mind over matter, mastery over thought, the purification of intellect, heart, spirit, innermost consciousness and the deeply concealed must all be exposed to the light. We become annoyed. These annoyances break down the positive chemical forces.

We have the law of karma to contend with. Every action has its reaction, its karmic results. As ye sow, so shall ye reap – cause and effect, the law of compensation. When we die, we will leave with our habits, flaws, and unresolved business. Facing the lions, you're cleaning house for both this life and the next.

We all learned much as we examined ourselves in the temples of the Other Side and our reactions were put through the microscope. One by one, we confronted lions of anger, pride, deceit, greed, criticism, stubbornness, deviousness, hatred, selfishness, laziness, lying, dishonesty, envy, jealousy, delusion, malice, slander, avarice, aversion, fear, arrogance, negligence, denial, deception, irritability, impatience, doubt, resentment, cowardice, self pity, gossip, ingratitude, vanity, guilt, conceit, intolerance, possessiveness, prejudice, insincerity, hypocrisy, worry, anxiety ... the list is endless.

******

ELEVENTH STEEP   To the TEMPLE OF REDEMPTION

First Station GRACE is the "perfume of God" ennobling one on the Earth path with beauty and graciousness. Its influence portrays obedience to the divine law of universal love.

Second Station SIMPLICITY. Simplicity is profound understanding, free of complexity, in response to spiritual guidance.

Third Station FORGIVENESS is the giving over to the God power in radiant understanding, a cleansing force that frees resentment, criticism and guilt.

Fourth Station TRUST. Trust is the opening of self to be filled with God's supply of goodness, love and guidance. It is a resting in faith that all that is needed will be supplied.

Fifth Station COOPERATION. Cooperation is an active realization that one is part of all others and must operate in harmony with God, nature, his fellow man and himself in flexible consideration of opinion, influences and forces.

Sixth Station EXPECTANCY. Expectancy is that which is looked forward to with interest in reasonable assurance of fulfillment through the rightness of conditions.

******

TEMPLE OF REDEMPTION

MIRIAM Inspired and fortified by all we've seen and experienced in the Area of Devotion, we ascend along the 11th Steep in a devoted resolution to bring the heavenly supply to manifestation in our Earth life. As we learn in our tests in the Stations of the 11th Steep, this requires grace, the color of rose bisque, the 11th Ray of the Spiritual Arc of Purple. Grace is the strength of gentleness, the quiet unobtrusive love of God in action that has been called the perfume of God's love. Grace is giving in delicate, tender strength. It's retiring of the ego that the power of spirit may manifest. Many who've faced traumas have felt the subtle blessing of God's grace.

We're happy to have our need supplied in the first station, in the beautiful effulgence of God's grace, where at-one-ment with self creates a great simplicity within us. There's a strange element about simplicity, for in spiritual life and its expression of simplicity, there's a great profundity. Jesus was the simplest of men through the depths and the heights of his being, the breadth of his understanding, the extent of his power – think of it.

The clarifying of simplicity reveals our need for forgiveness, and brings us to the Station of Forgiveness, the next station we're permitted to enter. In forgiveness one learns trust is also a required element. Forgiveness brings trust to birth, as it were, and as all needs are supplied in that blessed kingdom of light, one enters the security of this Station of Trust.

Here one experiences need to cooperate with the divine power given for his use in these stations of testing, learning and becoming, and here one is imbued with the uplift of gratitude to respond. This impetus gives us entrée to the next station – cooperation, where we find that cooperation always leads to fulfillment and to hunger and thirst for ongoing. And we do have to cooperate with spiritual law. This propelling urge brings us to the Station of Expectancy.

CONNIE How does fulfillment fit in?

MIRIAM Well, cooperation brings the experience of fulfillment, doesn't it? It's on the wings of accepted responsibility that we go to the Temple of Redemption. We reach the Temple of Redemption, climbing upward, up the Steeps of power. You know when we come to the Temple of Redemption.

MARY As we approached the dome-shaped temple, these words inscribed in letters of flowing light are shown us as seekers on the path: "Legions of angelic powers wait upon the soul and guide it to the Mount of Vision, where by the grace of God, it can walk in simple faith, trusting in the invisible hand that points the way. Every day the voice calls to our intuitive consciousness: "Onward and upward is the way to attain development and develop spiritual sight and hearing. You and you alone place your feet upon the path of enlightenment."

The voice rings out: "Arise, seekers on the Path, and the Master will lead you on the search for self-mastery. There are no material physical steps by which to reach awareness of your soul. You need not relinquish anything to recognize your own divine spirit. Believe this statement: 'Illumination comes through adoration; adoration comes through prayer; prayer comes by acceptance of who we are and why we are here.'"

We pray to be able to live in exaltation and sunshine on the lighted path. Sweetness of Spirit radiates outwardly in vibrations which, more subtle than the vibrations of light or heat, are also more potent. They are more powerful in their action of conditions and in the impressions they connect to others, more powerful than the highest force we know.

Chemical changes are not more absolutely demonstrable than are these. They act on conditions and dreary circumstances as the sun's rays act upon the snow to melt and dissipate, or as light acts upon darkness that flees before the sun. So all dark conditions fade before the vibrations of the radiant, trusting and serenely sweet spirit; spirit is the one most powerful force. I ask you to accept and live with self control and a radiant faith that grasps ideal conditions and colors life with the love of the Master. Bless you.

MIRIAM WILLIS When we reach this spot there's a turning backward in gratitude for the many blessings. experiences and initiations we've had. There are those and many who have not tasted of the above blessings. May we share some of this bounty.

MARY In all these power stations of the Steep, the soul has experienced two aspects: his attainment and his lacks. And the door of reformation opens before him to the Temple of Redemption.

The temple is revealed as a great dome, perfectly round, and in color from deep violet-purple at its base through ascending hues into the red-purples, amethysts on to ruby and rose with a hovering canopy of iridescent beauty ever moving in a changing light-filled delicate rainbow tint that bathes and encircles the temple dome, much as clouds embrace the mountains. From this canopy of power, most ethereal music flows like an elusive dance in exquisite rhythm. Awed by the continuity of the temple's great solidity and ephemeral beauty, one is drawn into its embrace and is enfolded within it.

We didn't feel as though we entered; rather, the temple seemed to reach out to enfold us. Every possibility of doubt, failure or discouragement dropped away in the restoring force of this experience, hope filled with a realization of the infinite love that never fails the earnest seeker. Tears of cleansing gratitude well up from the depths of one's being, aligning one's bodies and motives with purifying action.

One stands before the unfolding of oneself and the divine redemptive force that recreates unto at-one-ment of being with integrating power up to the level of one's conscious attainment. One joins the company of those who, like himself, have experienced these initiations. Together with our guides and teachers, we join in a march of peace for the redemption of all mankind.

You have many needs within your surface being, only one of which is to learn self acceptance and self understanding. The human mind is a willful thing. If it's worthwhile for you to lose all the unhappiness you've known and to find all the joys you've longed for, then turn your life over to the great intelligence. Let it tell you what to do.

How shall you apply what you've nightly learned? Like all parts of truth, this is very simple: you need only make an effort to remind yourself to do it, because the doing itself comes effortlessly. Soon you'll prove that living by the Creator's laws produces harmony so great you're renewed and relaxed from the common frustrations you've so long lived with.

Open yourself, let go to express happiness and love. You surely know the power that carries you beyond the doorway of the material plane is love; otherwise the temples of learning couldn't be contacted.

The meditation in which you seek your own identity with God is motivated by love. The deeds you perform to help others on the physical plane are caused by love. When you've gained a constant awareness of love, you've gained all there is in your world. The higher spiritual round on which you stand today enables you to perceive the reality of the law of vibration, and to trace to it results whose cause had before been conjectural.

The words spoken in a room are photographed, as it were, on the air, and can be read afterward by one whose perceptions are sufficiently developed. The "atmosphere" of a room, in its spiritual sense, is as in much fact as is the quality of air. "Mind is designed for mastery." In this more magnetic, intense and responsive atmosphere lie undreamed of possibilities of beauty and happiness. Herein peace is attained.

With all its flaws, faults and hypocrisies and the things we regret in ourselves and in our brothers, a great light has been held, and we help to hold it, for in the Master we follow, there is this marvelous bridge of at-one-ment; there is the overcoming of vexations, the overcoming of karma in redemptive power of the Christ.

MIRIAM WILLIS It's always there, flowing from the heart of God. We can draw upon its power and make it our own. All this contains within it a redemptive force and a transforming power that is yours and mine. And this calm brings about the reconciliation within ourselves and with each another. This is the vision we need to hold for the chaos of our physical world.

VIOLET Has there ever been a time when the people of the world have been more filled with the terrible lack of reconciliation?

MIRIAM ALBPLANALP Over against that, has there ever been a time when more effort toward reconciliation has been and is being put forth?

MARY When we're thinking of the 9th Plane Temple of Redemption, we're thinking of the wonder of the power of God that lifts us out of any situation that lacks harmony, unification, reconciliation, restoration – all these qualities of redemption – and we look up with joy in our hearts to the inflowing power, and say, "In Him all powers are reconciled. I am aligned in that power of the Christ into a unified, harmonious whole in body, soul and spirit."

This is the gift of the Lord Jesus – at-one-ment with our selves, at-one-ment with God, at-one-ment with our fellow man. Take the gift. Keep it in the golden casket of your love. Shield it from the storms of the darkness of the world, that its flame may rise high and touch the very heart of God, and reach out to warm the souls of men.

GENE I was very aware in this temple of the colors of the 11th and 12th rays of the Spiritual Arc of Green.

RALPH The 11th Ray is a light yellow green with a soft light blue midray. It's one of my favorite colors. It means "at-one-ment with self, peace, and joy of accomplishment."

GENE This ray soars very high in vibration.

MIRIAM WILLIS Indeed it does. And as we know, more yellow in the green adds enlightenment to the basic energy, and the blue midray brings an added spiritual quality.

ANDREW The 12th Ray of the Spiritual Arc of Green is a beautiful ray. The delicate yellow green that means at-one-ment with God brings illumination. It's the height of growth in the Green Arc.

MIRIAM WILLIS More and more light is added as the soul seeks increasing advancement. The seeker utilizes physical energy and effort to accept challenges and refine himself with more and more spiritual light, as he grows in balance. Illumination guides his steps as the seeker listens to the inner voice of spirit and follows guidance.

MARY With the thought of inflowing light, power and love of the divine, let us brighten up the colors, bring them into greater maturity. There's a force that's created from the Other Side when you say to the invisibles, "Help me to send this Color to someone."

MIRIAM We need this reconciliation so many times within our own being. And we find that the practice of meditation and prayer, our use of Color, and our faithful climbing of the Channel help bring the balance that creates reconciliation – harmony between all the many parts of the intricacies of our being.

We have the consolation, the realization that we're not limited to the thought of human attainment, but that we have the inflow of the resurrected Christ, that bridge twixt Heaven and Earth, which quickens all our powers and causes us to ignite the flame of the Christ within, with the power and transcendence of the great Christ who triumphed over all human weaknesses.

VIOLET Great missionary spirit has been born through the outreach of brotherhood. Then receptivity— we feel the reaction of receiving.

LOLA I had a vision: a web like a huge high cylinder, almost opaque, as if there were a light inside. It was not a shiny force, but you could tell from the light underneath that there was great intensity of light within. The cylinder rose, and then there was revealed greater light yet, and this seemed to continue as if we were not quite ready. I couldn't stand the full intensity of the light.

HELEN VON GEHR My vision was of someone holding a torch. It moved forward; there was no color with it; it was like a statue come to life.

MARY To me that would mean "a change," bringing it down to life, but your muted colors would say it would be a glorious change, because you must have gone into silver, did you not? When you gave me the picture, dear, it looked like fish scales floating in the air, iridescent silver. . . the fish, the coloring and everything came to me as spiritual life. That's an Egyptian symbol.

MARGARET It wasn't that the ceremony we experienced in the temple was different, but the words were slightly different. For instance, what I brought back was the heavenly guides asked me what my dearest wish was, which happened to coincide with things I wanted to promise for the coming new year. It seemed the questions were slightly different than I've ever experienced before. Now was that my imagination?

MARY That was your development of a year. It might have been a little harder to answer, too. If we step up a little ways, you know, we're on the level of consciousness we're not used to. Yes, it could be different in that way.

LORNA Mary, what do you think of people who believe in hellfire and punishment, who believe that the end of the world is coming, that God will destroy the world because its people are so evil?

MARY I can't conceive that the great architect of the universe who designed this world and all its intricacies and all its beauty would throw the creation he made into the flames.

BERNARD The phrase "end of the world" has been mistranslated. There are biblical references, of course, but the meaning is not an actual destruction of the world. Instead, it really means "the Consummation of the Age," the finishing up of a major cycle when the harvest of souls is sown and the wheat is separated from the tares.

VIOLET "Many are called but few are chosen."

MARY No soul is ever lost. We're given infinite chances. But I think our hearts burn with sorrow, and that we do have to redeem ourselves, we do have to undo what we've done. But if we can do it here, acknowledge, know ourselves, forgive ourselves, come back into the realm of self respect and grow taller in our stance, looking up to God, I believe we're forgiven before we go. I think we're not denied. The earnestness of our heart takes us through, so that then we don't need to have all these long delays after death.

LORNA How exactly does one avoid the long delays?

MARY By doing the work while here on earth, taking stock of the plan of one's life, how it has been and is being lived, becoming conscious, handling the reasons for your incarnation, coming to grips with and resolving issues, making amends, forgiving, releasing. In each experience given you in these temples on the Planes, you as an evolving soul develop faculties and capacities, leaving less to be attained when you enter life eternal, giving you, the seeker, celestial recompense.

HELEN MARSH I had a vision of a building, a large dome in the center with two smaller ones, as in a mosque. It's alabaster, a hue symbolic of new beginnings, and represents embracing mindfulness, wellbeing and an atmosphere that's pure.

MICHAEL Mindfulness - that's our Eightfold Path.

RALPH Alabaster again: a vision of a large, golden-colored alabaster stone shaped like a cameo that was held by two angel hands.

MARY That stone is faith at the top of the temple.

GLENN I was seeing a lot of color in the temple we went to. I was seeing this soft grey pink lavender.

MARGARET That's the 8th Ray of the Spiritual Arc of Purple, and it means harmony.

MIRIAM WILLIS The stabilizing force of the grey, the controlling vibration of the blue, and the warming energy of the pink merge to provide harmony. Harmony gives the power to be in rhythm from wherever you are to be in the love rhythm of the universe.

MARGARET During meditation tonight I had glimpses and impressions of beautiful autumn colors. One was part of a temple, where it seemed a series of madonna-like figures were lifting up babies under a kind of moon or half moon. Would there be a Thanksgiving service over there, in which they gave thanks for these youngsters?

MARY Could easily be. Well, I'll tell you, it's a Hindu rite, if nothing else. The last born is always taken at this time of year, harvest time, to the temple. Usually our Thanksgiving falls at the same time as their Hindu rite, the last week of November. Everyone brings food to the temple, food that's ripened and the most perfect they can give. They bring their last born and hold the babies up to be blessed. They walk under this golden half moon that they say almost all children in the nation have been carried under. That half moon is over their head, and that is supposed to be what I might call an umbrella to keep them safe from harm.

They say that sometimes, whether it's a harem girl or a girl from a house of nobility, she will bring both her firstborn and last born, because she wants both of them blessed. She may hide that other child in her robes, but she manages to let the little face look up at the golden half moon. They are very sure that it gives them protection for life!

******

REVIEW XIII
MARY'S ENLIGHTENED TEACHINGS
COLOR AND THE PLANES

How did Mary received the enlightened teachings of Color and the Planes of Heaven?

When she was thirty years old, Mary had a severe case of pneumonia followed by a staph infection, and was bedridden, unable to walk, for more than a year. The Mayo Brothers, who were friends of Mary's physician husband, and a number of other leading doctors examined her. Charles Mayo even declared, "This girl will never walk again," adding, "and I can prove it."

Says Mary, "But then, one day I dreamed I was moving. When I woke, I was stretched out on the window seat by the bay window. I had walked there. Next I knew, I was back in bed. I woke and thought, that didn't happen, I just imagined it. But the same event occurred over and over."

It took nearly another year before Mary was completely rehabilitated. During this time, she was given, from the Other Side, both the Color and the Planes courses, as well as guidance in learning ancient languages.

Over a period of 20 years, Mary and her husband, Dr. George Weddell, discovered that color healed others physically, mentally, emotionally and spiritually. Once they were assured thorough practical experience of color's efficacy, the Weddells began teaching. Mary's first classes, held in Bel Air and Beverly Hills, California, consisted of 100 doctors and dentists. In time, she had a group of students from England and France who came to Southern California every other year to absorb her teachings.

******

> TWELFTH STEEP   To the TEMPLE and AREA OF REBIRTH AND RENEWAL, TEMPLE OF SANCTIFICATION, TEMPLE OF SUSPENSION, TEMPLE OF CHRIST CONSCIOUSNESS
>
> First Station STEADFASTNESS. Steadfastness is standing firm in the qualities attained thus far. The Seeker becomes constant, resolute, and unswerving, rooted in flexible strength.
>
> Second Station   CONFIDENCE. Confidence is a state of mind characterized by reliance on quiet self-possession, positive in the certitude that one has access to wisdom.
>
> Third Station FAITHFULNESS. Faithfulness is persevering and thorough in performance of duty; loyal in affection; worthy of trust.
>
> Fourth Station   GENTLENESS. Gentleness refines the vulgar or coarse, tames, mollifies and softens in quiet patience.
>
> Fifth Station TENDERNESS. Tenderness is a state of sensitive apperception and consideration of feelings; delicate strength; compassion and kindness.
>
> Sixth Station   BEAUTY. Beauty is the subtle enchantment in essence and concept of ideal perfection of form, color or quality.

TEMPLE OF SUSPENSION

From the Temple of Redemption, where we were cleansed and restored, we ascended toward the Stations of the Twelfth Steep. The tests we undergo there reveal our innermost needs. The first test is Steadfastness; next Confidence, then Faithfulness; Gentleness; Tenderness; and Beauty. The fulfilling of these qualities penetrate to the depths and height of our being, and we feel the need of help in our search, for the level of rebirth on this 9th Plane is high indeed.

Spiritual unfoldment is an endless journey of progression. And yet, a realization should come during the experiences of the 9th Plane that brings the greater reality of integration of spirit within our being than we've had before.

ESTHER BARNES I brought through a recall of a beautiful field of luminous silver poppies. Farther on, there was a large structure of some kind that was also very luminous. It had some turrets on it and it sat on a gentle knoll. Below it was a lovely area with sparsely grown trees.

MARY That's the Temple of Suspension, the south wing, dear, of the Temple of Suspension. It is turreted and of luminous material.

JANE After a lesson in the Temple of Suspension, I was taken to one of the temples that contain the Akashic Records. I remember Mary said how at a certain point we may be shown aspects of our past lives and those of our loved ones so as to better understand something that's needed for our development and our Plan of Life.

Throughout my life, I always had the feeling I didn't love my parents enough, even though I was a good child who appreciated, honored and respected my parents. After I married, we lived close by in the same town, so my parents were always a big part of my life. In their declining years, I cared for both my mother and my father until they passed on. Despite my devotion to them, I always felt there was something missing in my capacity to love them. I didn't love them enough, or I didn't "really love" them.

The reason I had this feeling was explained to me in the Akashic Records, when I saw some past lives of both my parents. At last I understood so much, both about them and about myself. And in an instant, I felt a great surge, an enormous burst of huge love for my parents, the kind of feeling that had always eluded me. The love that I had always found wanting in myself came into fullness, finally completely expressed. I know I'm not explaining this well. But it was such a remarkable experience, it gave me an enlightenment that swelled my heart and brought a feeling of immeasurable joy and peace. After that, I will never be the same.

*****

AREA and TEMPLE OF CHRIST CONSCIOUSNESS

The Area and Temple of Christ Consciousness are contained in a diamond shaped area on the right side of the chart of the 9th Plane.

MARY Here a teacher told us, "Mind is the master power that molds and makes. Man is mind. Evermore he takes the tool of thought, and shaping what he wills, brings forth a thousand joys, a thousand ills. He thinks in secret, and it comes to pass. Environment is but his looking glass."

The plan of life, as it works through those who've come to understand it, find it begins as a dream, a vision, a desire; then the seeker finds himself reaching out to attain it, and finally comes the fulfillment. As fulfillment in our lives is the ultimate aim, it is only when we begin setting the laws of God in motion for us rather than against us that we begin experiencing this fulfillment of our dreams.

When as children we saw the beautiful and varied colored tinsel balls hanging on the Christmas tree, we were fascinated with what we thought they were – iridescent worlds that held wonder and enchantment, worlds of color in which we could see ourselves and the flames of candles reflected, glistening, glowing promises of fun and happiness. But as we grew older and knowledge destroyed imagination, we recognized those former wonders for what they were, little tinsel shells that break easily, hollow shapes that looked deeper and more rewarding than they were. And so we turned to more sophisticated things to answer our needs, to a thousand other things that seemed to bring us the quiet restfulness and assurance we needed.

But these are seldom enough. The real essence of peace, the unfailing key to the discovery of the silence of peace, lies within each of us. As our physical boundaries are squeezed and narrowed, as we reach higher up, farther out and deeper down, we lose our breathless fascination with the unknown. The tinsel of our imaginative dreams is broken, and we must look somewhere else for the peace that was destroyed. We must look to the soul within ourselves, the infinite creative energy, we then will be able to face the potential of this swiftly moving life, and reach that illusive frontier, the all embracing peace, a touch of universal understanding.

JUDITH   I had a decidedly numinous experience in my night work in this temple. I saw two large plastic bags packed with items that I realized needed to be thrown out. Each bag was in a different location in a house which was supposedly my house, although I didn't recognize ever having been in this house that was supposed to be mine. I was willing to throw out one of the plastic bags, but hesitant about letting go of the other one. A guide urged and encouraged me to throw the second bag out but I kept resisting and making excuses. I just desperately wanted to hang onto it, even though the better move was to throw it out. But I just couldn't do it!

ANDREW   That makes sense. With the first bag, she was ready to get rid of the old, but the other bag, she wasn't ready to let go yet; she was still clinging to old molds.

JUDITH   Believe me, I'm working on letting go... and discovering what it is I need to relinquish.

*****

AREA and TEMPLE OF REBIRTH AND RENEWAL

From the Temple of Christ Consciousness, we were taken to the Temple of Rebirth and Renewal, where we received instructions in "thought building."

MARY   As I was seeking ardently to picture the sanctuary of my hidden life, on a hillside at the edge of a forest in a secluded valley, I was shown my self. I recognized I was entering the path of light the seeker must take to find his way into the Temple of Rebirth and Renewal.

Suddenly, the heavens became filled with light. My consciousness was caught up into a realm radiant with that light which never was on Earth land or sea. Gradually I realized the pressure of an angelic being that was doubtless responsible for my elevated state of mind.

From the teacher's mind to mine, there began to flow a stream of ideas concerning the life force and the consciousness of universal love, a love endeavoring to change coldness, bitterness and criticism into warmth and sweetness through faith in our daily living, and faith in the night work in the temples of Heaven.

Filled with transcendent happiness, we hold within our hearts a knowledge of renewal, as once more we're on our way with a desire to reach spiritual growth. With this growth, the seeker becomes a catalyst and an alchemist, for he takes dross and refines it until it becomes gold. He becomes a master craftsman in reforming lives, for he has faith in God and himself.

The seeker has become aware of his place in creation. He has sacrificed nothing except the human habit of thinking fearful thoughts, including doubt, criticism, worry, envy, and resentment. The seeker has proven to himself that throughout the universe runs a great magnetic current—God's love for mankind.

In the Temple of Rebirth and Renewal, the seeker learns to combine his forces in unity of purpose, to distinguish, discriminate, separate, and unite in persistence of personality and his individual comprehension of his life and character. Here he identifies himself in knowledge he has attained, realizing the things he knows and the things he must seek further to know. Thus he grows in soul consciousness and realizes his soul's identity with God. His purpose in development is more clearly defined. Balance is his watchword and his shield.

The colors that are given us for development in this temple are: nile green, sea foam green, rose henna and many shades of rose, climbing to the heights.

GEORGE Nile green is the color of awareness.

RALPH The 10th Ray of the Spiritual Arc of Green is sea foam green.

GENE This ray means "awareness of sowing and reaping, the Law of Compensation; expanding in conscious understanding."

GLENN The ray signifies the relentless rhythm of ocean tides: "as a man soweth, so shall he reap," cause and effect, karma, what goes around comes around.

MIRIAM WILLIS This is a balancing ray that encourages growth, challenges one to new goals, and helps you recognize unrewarding patterns. It helps us to be receptive to inflowing currents of soul wisdom to replace ego-centered concepts.

ESTHER BARNES Using this ray expands higher consciousness and transforms thinking.

HELEN MARSH I've been hoping for a certain thing to happen in my Earth life. In the Temple of Rebirth and Renewal this week, I saw a series of large photographs in the 11 x 17 size, surrounded by the sea foam green color of the 10th Ray of the Spiritual Arc of Green. Two of the photos were of myself and a telephone. I kept wanting to fuse these photos together, because they were disjointed but obviously belonged as a unified unit. All they needed was to be stitched together and they would make one excellent photo. Then right after meditation the day following this experience, it dawned on me, in a sudden flash, exactly what I need to do to manifest the thing I've been hoping to happen. It was such a revelation, I can't tell you!

VIOLET That telephone is an interesting symbol ... obviously it's communication with her inner self. Of course, everything we experience on the Other Side is communicating with our inner selves, but Helen's experience seems to go even a step farther.

MARY Just as only by much searching and mining are gold and diamonds obtained, we can find every truth connected with our being if we will dig deep into the mine of our soul.

For we make our own character; we are molder of our lives and the builder of our destiny. We may unerringly prove, if we will watch, control, and alter our thoughts, tracing their effects upon our life and circumstances, upon others, linking cause and effect by patient practice and investigation, and utilizing every experience, even to the most trivial everyday occurrence, as a means of obtaining that knowledge of ourselves.

MIRIAM WILLIS "The wise man, he whose thoughts are controlled and purified, makes the winds and storms of the soul obey."

MARY This Area of Rebirth and Renewal on the 9th Plane is a very high demand, shall I say, on both our Earth life and our Heaven life. And so we go back many times to discover and apply the revelations to build the power needed for fulfillment.

All the help we're able to receive is given, and life itself becomes the great revealer. So we're quickened to look for the subtle things, the apparently small things that need transforming into rebirth. We're counseled to watch and pray, to live in confident faith, to accept in love and to lift in joyous hope, knowing that all things are possible in the light and Color of the great creative power of God's love and wisdom. Ask and ye shall receive; seek and ye shall find; knock and it will be opened to you.

Happy New Year to all of you blessed people.

*****

TEMPLE OF SANCTIFICATION

This ascendance requires a deep realization of our responsibilities, the fulfilling of which creates the spiritual growth necessary for such high attainment. We search out the particular qualities we variously need. These we discover through testing on the heavenly Path and in the challenges of our Earth lives.

Each life must pass through many varied changes, and each change is a great experience – an adventure and a going from darkness into light, an evolution, a portrayal of the effulgence of the life force.

MIRIAM Thus in the Temple of Sanctification we go to one of the many entrances. The interior followed a spiraled pattern in brilliant rainbows magnificent to behold. This supply of Color is so lavish that one is awed into the realization that responsibility is given from above and responded to by man's degree of receptivity, fulfilled through the action of his will. This causes his faith to be reestablished in deep resolve and gratitude.

As everyone present responds, a great paean of praise breaks the silence.

*****

REVIEW XIV
PLANES 1-10

THE 1ST PLANE interpenetrates the Earth at its center and extends out far beyond the surface of the physical Earth. The outer surface of the 1st Plane upon which its inhabitants dwell is many leagues out in space beyond the surface of the Earth. This plane is instinctive, instructive and expressive; it is a plane of adjustment and expansion, the plane of examination, also known as the plane of development. Here, we are confronted by certain questions: What is our degree of spiritual development? How many fundamental issues of spirit have we absorbed? How much do we practice spiritual principles? Do I really know myself? Do I know my purpose in life?

THE 2ND PLANE is the Afterlife home of discarnate secularists, atheists, agnostics, materialists and unbelievers. It is a moral plane; that is, dwellers face moral issues and make decisions to do things over again. Important parts of this plane are five principles in five temples that begin with "Re:" Revelation, Remembrance, Retribution, Renunciation, and Redemption. (In Greek, re means going into, as to contemplate). On the 2nd Plane, one is in an area of instruction, designed to provide for the neglects and failures of life.

THE 3RD PLANE: Beginning of the Kingdom of God. Homes and religious houses of worship proliferate on this plane.

THE 4TH PLANE is the citadel of fourth dimensional thinking, cosmic consciousness, and self mastery.

THE 5TH PLANE is where dreams and visions are revealed to the awakened soul. Spiritual sensing quickens as does creative thinking. The test of faith here is how much of nonessentials have I relinquished? One of our greatest tests is answering the questions: who am I, and why am I here.

THE 6TH PLANE is a pivotal plane — the mystic gate where we learn to balance our spiritual and physical bodies.

THE 7TH PLANE is where all previous tests are repeated in preparation for the 8th Plane. It is a plane of divine imagination, perseverance, and desire to share. This plane represents hidden life, the reality of unspoken thoughts, feelings and emotions.

THE 8TH PLANE is the work of the Eightfold Path. Here we receive training in setting aside the smaller self, discipline in overcoming self and circumstances.

THE 9TH PLANE is steeper going than the previous planes. We depend more on ourselves, less on receiving outside help. This plane applies especially to walking in the light of understanding, where we survey the death and resurrection of the self in light and love. Spiritual balance, reality of message, discernment between imagination and truth, and integration of the spiritual powers of sight and hearing are aspects of this plane.

THE 10TH PLANE is the last plane on which we work as an incarnated soul. We unfold on the higher planes as discarnate souls. The action of the disciple on the 10th Plane is selfless life of consecrated service, the height of human earthly attainment brought into focus in service for the Kingdom of Heaven on Earth. The previous nine planes developed character; the 10th plane develops consciousness.

There are many planes and heavenly dimensions beyond these first ten planes. How many? Undoubtedly thousands, millions, billions, likely an infinite number, more than any human mind can begin to grasp. The highest plane of reality may be unfathomable, but the purpose of humanity is to continually progress towards that goal.

OTHER 9TH PLANE TEMPLES

In addition to the aforementioned Temples and Areas of the Steeps, the class had lessons and tests in additional 9th Plane temples:

TEMPLE OF WORSHIP

ESTHER BARNES During meditation, I saw great Persian gates. It was as if there were endless numbers of angels waiting to open the gate. And later I saw just the head of a woman. Her eyes – beautiful large eyes, were just looking out in a very loving way. I asked to go in. It was magnificent, so great.

MARY It's the Temple of Worship, dear. There are many gates we enter, because we are of many faiths. They all go through, eventually, the same gate to God, open the same door to God.

KATIE BASINSKI Monday, I saw three crosses that were almost as if cut from stone. They were an unusual shape and had an arch behind them.

MARY The Temple of Worship. We come up to the big gateway there and those crosses stand above the gate and look down at us.

GEORGE Is the Temple of Worship for all faiths?

MARY No man is denied a place to worship. So in whatever form men of other nations worship God, they can go to the great Temple of Worship. We go to this Temple for training.

Within the Temple of Worship are many small temples where we sometimes go. I will say to you, "Oh, that's in the great Temple of Worship, it's a left corridor, or somewhere, south corridor." I try to name it so that if we've been there, you could place it in your consciousness.

GERTRUDE I think I can place a temple in my consciousness more easily when you tell us about it, but I wish I could place it without your help! Still, I do experience a few things that help me identify where we've been.

MIRIAM WILLIS One step at a time, dear. We're all seekers on the Path.

MARY I think that the greatest revelation to a teacher who teaches this truth is that you see within the soul of the students all the activities and what they've brought back from the sights they've seen.

I tell you, I believe the day will come when your full consciousness will be revealed to you. Psychologically, the teachers have tried to do that throughout the years, revealing to each human being what's lodged within the consciousness that they don't realize – nor do they use that space. It's as if one had turned the lid down on a small empty box and stowed away within it something that is unpleasant, or something that is a jewel of memory. So we do all have these boxes that can be used. Some have never been opened, especially the spiritual boxes. But our experiences in our auras reveal all that is there and all that has improved and regenerated.

VIRGINIA This came to me as a dream. The light was so bright it was blinding. It looked like an overexposed photograph – too much light. I was coming out of something; I was in a small boat going over water. It didn't seem very wide. I know dreams have three aspects, but I was puzzled how to interpret what I'd seen, where I'd been.

MARY Let us take a personal or psychological viewpoint. Would you not say that you were on water, and you were protected in a boat, but you truly didn't know your way?

VIRGINIA I didn't know my way, true, but there was someone there to receive me, a guide, a teacher.

MARY That gives it the spiritual aspect. If there's a guiding thought or a presence that guides, then you are in a higher aspect of learning and thinking.

VIRGINIA There was definite manifestation in the physical, too. which occurred later.

MARGARET This probably means she had a test on the Other Side, symbolized by her dream, and then she had a matching Earth test., manifested in the physical.

PATTI This was either a dream or a vision: the entire circle of the horizon was covered with buildings. It was dark outside, but illuminated inside. Then all the light that was inside came to the center and distilled into very large dewdrops of light. Then all the dewdrops lifted like a fountain of light up to Heaven.

MARY That's the Chamber of Illumination in the Temple of Worship.

MARGARET Saturday night I saw two towers, which I thought probably were the ones Lola had seen the week before. They were quite tall with gold domes, and they had lavender and purple stripes between the storeys. And there on the inside it was like amethyst glass going from the floor clear to the top with pieces of rose inset at various spots.

MARY Both Lola and you were in the Temple of Worship. The Temple of Worship incorporates many other temples where you go for your worship and your experience. These are the same, but different portions of the temple. You went to the tower.

LOLA I had seen that tower as almost translucent with a light within it.

MARY You two were together on that. Temple of Worship, Tower of Enlightenment.

HELEN MARSH This morning I brought back that a group of us was gathered in the temple, standing around. We stepped back and saw that the floor was inlaid with tile. It had a star motif, outlined in beautiful colors. I believe this is the Temple of Worship.

MARY Yes, and the star is amber. You were there last night, Temple of Worship.

RUBY During meditation, I had the impression of having been in a temple, but all I could see was the front of it – a beautiful stained glass window in a sunburst pattern.

MARY Yes. That's the Temple of Worship, dear. We were there last night. We do reflect our colors. When we see something translucent as we approach it, it reflects us. Walk up, here's nothing but a translucent door, and all of a sudden it's filled with the light of yourself. And then we pass those black mirrors that we go into in our testing rooms, and sometimes we think it could not possibly be that "my aura is like that." Then we go to the next room, and we go and see the reality, and we're quite sad for some time.

You know, I always thought, "I wonder why I didn't go to the beautiful one." You take the last and carry the memory away, but it isn't so. As we've seen, there's the bitter with the sweet, and the sweet comes first. It's sort of a temptation, an invitation to go on. Now you don't need to go on, but something just tells you you'd better go into the next corridor, and at the end you see. You walk along these black mirrors – ebony, they seem like, and what they're made of I don't know. I don't think I've ever asked. They shine like marble; they're mirrors. The depth of it – it's a black mirror, that 's all I can say.

In that is reflected all your auric colors. And you yourselves, one by one as you've walked in that corridor there, you've taken a look at yourself; every one of you has come out and said, "You know, Mary, I've improved." So with that much improvement, I was quite encouraged.

*****

TEMPLE OF WISDOM AND UNDERSTANDING

Only by patience, practice, and ceaseless importunity can a man enter the door of the Temple of Wisdom and Understanding.

******

AREA and TEMPLE OF CONSCIOUS SENSITIVITY AND AREA OF VIBRATORY REFINEMENT

Only going through the Temple of Conscious Sensitivity and the Area of Vibratory Refinement can man become a part of Universal Brotherhood and live in extended consciousness.

The intuitive path leads the seeker into the Temple of Conscious Sensitivity and the Area of Vibratory Refinement, where he receives spiritual education. And like any other knowledge offered, one's progress is according to his individual ability. You are the sum total of your own faith and awareness. No one holds you back or pushes you forward.

VIOLET As we approached the Temple of Conscious Sensitivity, there was a soft misty cloud before us. As it cleared, a most beautiful temple seemed to grow, and as it rose, more of this lovely structure revealed its coloring, blended in soft shell-like blue, with very gentle pinks and yellows through it, all hazy like the mist.

The temple had many slender columns along the front view which gave lightness. One couldn't tell of what it was made – marble, perhaps. Its substance was slightly mottled with the same colors, only a deeper shade.

Now all was clear, and it stood there still very mysterious and lovely. We were allowed to enter. The atmosphere gave us a sense of a power beyond us, attracting and impelling. The force created within us, seemingly from beyond our horizon, outside our natures, a lovely and beautiful attraction: of mother-of-pearl effect to our sight, of deliciousness to our taste, touching us in mystery and love, and to our ears, receptivity as a harmonious hum.

In this temple we were having our five senses raised to the point where they were lifted into spiritual sensing, seeing, hearing, smelling and tasting, until these avenues of communication with the divine become so delicately attuned that we truly reached this finer level of awareness. Like delicate instruments, we were being tuned, attuned and lifted into a radiant state of soul consciousness where one's physical five senses are raised in vibration until they become one's spiritual five senses. This is what was being done to us, in us and for us in this Temple.

When we're taken to the Temple of Conscious Sensitivity and to the Area of Vibratory Refinement, we realize that all our nature has given us a picture of the heavenly world, a paradise -- woods, fields, valleys, hills, rivers, clouds traveling across the sky. Light and darkness, sun and star, remind us Earth and Heaven are one, and that the value of our life is that it's a gift of God.

As we enter the temple we see displayed in flaming letters "Love; destroy fear; heal; banish hate. Love reveals Christ 's full power." These were the meanings of the flaming letters.

*****

TEMPLE OF EXPECTANCY

MARY The Temple of Expectancy first appears to us as a tube. We're puzzled by its unusual shape; we go all around it until eventually we find a staircase. We realize that this temple has a predominantly old Egyptian feel to it. The Egyptians were, early in the ages, some of the greatest people that God ever manifested to. Their seers were the noblest, and perhaps the most brilliantly developed of any of the priests of the far ages.

We were received in the temple's inner court, where we were told how expectation ranged in the field of mankind. Many thousands of years ago, the ancients knew man was made in the image of God. This was impressed on us, and we were told how we are still expected to develop into godlike creatures.

****

Following the Temple of Expectancy, we experienced tests, cleansing and energizing in "four cleansing temples:" the Temple of Revelation, Temple of Silence, Temple of Wisdom, and Temple of Dedication.

Other 9th Plane temples and areas we were privileged to visit include: Self Realization, Sensing, Spiritual Progression, Consecration, Omnipotence, Effulgence, Absorption, Universal Brotherhood, Extended Consciousness, Expanded Faith, Constructive Love, Healing Rays, Soul Communion, Intuition, Divine Inspiration, the Path, Sovereignty of the Godhead, Level of Universal Kinship, Life, Light, Love ... and more.

*****

REVIEW XV
MARY'S TEACHING ON THE THREE BODIES

The Spiritual Body is the garment of the soul, used while living here on Earth as a vehicle for the soul when the soul leaves the physical body in sleep. When not being used in the invisible form, the spiritual body dwells in the Heaven World. This spiritual body can be evoked through soul desire and raising vibrations, making it possible for a person to go to the Other Side in nightly sojourns to work toward development.

This spiritual body is universal. Each soul has its own, whose beauty and development is achieved by the living a life in accord with the fundamental laws of love. Emotions, thoughts and actions can be raised to the level of the consciousness of the spiritual body, the higher self. This brings peace, adjustment to life's trials, and spiritual growth. The Spirit is the active element of the Soul. There is in each person a white light which is 'the light of the soul.' One far enough advanced can see this light, the holy breath of spirit. The Soul gathers around itself elements that make it individual. To be conscious of our soul is to feel joy.

The mental, or thought body, maintains equilibrium or balance in the emotional realm between the physical and the spiritual, so that one can remain on the ray of power. Our soul consciousness is ahead of our Earth consciousness. We've used our mental body and our physical body, but our spiritual body has been unused to a great degree.

We seek to develop perfect balance in our three bodies, the physical, mental, and spiritual. Emotions, thoughts and actions can be raised to the level of the consciousness of the spiritual body, the higher self. Training through a teacher, knowledge gained in night work, caring and help given by one's guides, and the 'channel of divine power' are priceless gifts to balance control of the three bodies.

After our tests on the Other Side, we will always have Earth tests equal to our soul attainment in order to bring the bodies into balance. When they're in balance we are ready to go on to the next plane.

######

PART III

About Mary Weddell

About Author Jeanne Rejaunier

Reviews of the Planes books

Other Books by Jeanne Rejaunier

Review of THE BEAUTY TRAP, by Jeanne Rejaunier

ABOUT MARY WEDDELL

Mary Dies Weddell (1886-1980) was a remarkable woman whose teachings enlightened thousands of people in the United States and abroad. Musician (piano, organ, voice), poet, seer, philosopher and guru, Mary was the author of four published books; a specialist in Egyptology and hieroglyphics; linguist, particularly in Sanskrit, ancient Hebrew, Aramaic, and Greek. She was also one of the translators of the Dead Sea Scrolls.

******

AUTHOR JEANNE REJAUNIER

Jeanne Rejaunier graduated from Vassar College, Poughkeepsie, New York, and did postgraduate studies at the Sorbonne, Paris, the Universities of Florence and Pisa, Italy, the Goetheschule, Rome, and at UCLA. While a student at Vassar, she began a career as a professional model, and subsequently became an actress in Manhattan, Hollywood and Europe, appearing on and off Broadway, in films and television, on magazine covers internationally and as the principal in dozens of network television commercials.

Jeanne achieved international success with the publication of her first novel, **THE BEAUTY TRAP**, which sold over one million copies and became Simon and Schuster's fourth best seller of the year, the film rights to which were purchased outright by Avco-Embassy. Jeanne has publicized her books in national and international tours on three continents in five languages. Her writing has been extolled in feature stories in *Life, Playboy, Mademoiselle, Seventeen, BusinessWeek, Fashion Weekly, Women's Wear, W, McCalls, American Homemaker, Parade, Let's Live, Marie-Claire, Epoca, Tempo, Sogno, Cine-Tipo, Stern, Hola, The New York Times, The Los Angeles Times, The Washington Post*, and countless other publications. Jeanne has published more than two dozen books, most of which are available at online retailers and in bookstore chains.

Branching out as a filmmaker, Jeanne produced, directed, filmed, and edited the four hour documentary, **THE SPIRIT OF '56: MEETINGS WITH REMARKABLE WOMEN.**

*****

ALSO BY JEANNE REJAUNIER

The Planes of Heaven Series

PLANES OF THE HEAVENWORLD
EVERYTHING YOU ALWAYS WANTED TO KNOW ABOUT HEAVEN -- BUT DIDN'T KNOW WHERE TO ASK
THE KINGDOM OF HEAVEN AND 4TH DIMENSIONAL CONSCIOUSNESS
THE AFTERLIFE IN THE HERE AND NOW
LIVING IN ETERNITY NOW
THE EIGHTFOLD PATH AND THE 8TH PLANE OF HEAVEN

Other Nonfiction Titles

MY SUNDAYS WITH HENRY MILLER
HOLLYWOOD SAUNA CONFIDENTIAL
MODELING FROM THE GROUND UP
THE 50 BEST CAREERS IN MODELING
TITANS OF THE MUSES (with Noreen Nash)
THE PARIS DIET (with Noreen Nash & Monique de Warren)
ASTROLOGY FOR LOVERS (with Lu Ann Horstman)

Fiction

THE BEAUTY TRAP
THE MOTION AND THE ACT
AFFAIR IN ROME
MOB SISTERS
ODALISQUE AT THE SPA
EVERYBODY'S HUSBAND

All books are available in print and on all eBook platforms - for computer, tablet, eReader and smart phone.

*****

WHAT READERS ARE SAYING ABOUT THE PLANES OF HEAVEN SERIES

"A new universe of limitless visions and ideas."

"A totally new and exciting slant on spirituality."

"Groundbreaking ... unlike anything I've ever read before."

"What a priceless gift to share with those who are seeking a spiritual uplift!"

"How to prepare for your own transition by visiting the Planes of Heaven in the here and now."

"Discover how other Planes of Consciousness intertwine with our earthly life and vice versa."

"The descriptions and the wisdom imparted are amazing and will go a long way toward readers' understanding of life and the Afterlife. Having the verification of 50 different people is a wonderful assurance not only of what awaits us after we die, but will enrich our lives now as well."

"Ms. Rejaunier has handled this material with rare expertise and dedication."

"An excellent resource to any and all readers inquiring about 'what happens after death', as your energy (Soul) is released back into the Universe (Heaven)."

"This book offers a rare insight into Heaven."

"Any reader interested in spirituality, metaphysics, personal development, and self-help, would be fascinated by this interesting and compellingly written book."

CRITICS' REVIEWS - THE BEAUTY TRAP, BY JEANNE REJAUNIER

Here is a novel that can't miss, crammed with all the ingredients that make a blockbuster. **Publishers Weekly**

A startling closeup of the world's most glamorous business, an intensely human story. **The New York Times**

Jeanne Rejaunier has concocted a sexpourri of life among the mannequins that's spiked with all the ingredients of a blockbuster bestseller. **Playboy**

A fascinating inside story of the most glamorous girls in the business, absorbing to read. **California Stylist**

A powerful novel that takes off like 47 howitzers. **San Fernando Valley (CA) Magazine**

New York's most sought after women find themselves having to make desperate decisions that will affect their very lives. **Wilmington (DE) News Journal**.

The novel is rich in esoteric commercial lore about modeling. **Saturday Review**

Possibly the most honest novel to appear by a female writer in the past decade. **Literary Times**

Crammed with all the ingredients of a blockbuster. ..Beasts in the Beauty Jungle... authentic, searing exposé. **London Evening News**

Miss Rejaunier is most interesting when she goes behind the scenes in the modeling world. **Detroit Free Press**

If a male author had written *The Beauty Trap*, he'd be hanged by the thumbs. **UPI**

Made in the USA
San Bernardino, CA
01 May 2020